HOW TO PICK
A FAMILY FLICK

CHRIS HICKS

DESERET BOOK COMPANY
SALT LAKE CITY, UTAH

Library of Congress Cataloging-in-Publication Data

Hicks, Chris, 1948–
    How to pick a family flick / Chris Hicks.
        p.   cm.
    ISBN 0-87579-708-3
    1. Motion pictures—Catalogs.   2. Video recordings—Catalogs.
3. Motion pictures—Plots, themes, etc.   4. Family recreation—Film
catalogs.   I. Title.
PN1998.H54   1993
016.79143'75—dc20   93-13052
                                                                            CIP

Printed in the United States of America

10   9   8   7   6   5   4   3   2   1

CONTENTS

CONTENTS

VIDEO RECOMMENDATIONS

...

A GUIDE TO FAMILY FLICKS

INTRODUCTION

In May of 1988, in response to my review of *Rambo III* in the *Deseret News,* I received a pair of telephone calls from readers — back-to-back calls, both asking why the film was rated R.

The crux of the first phone conversation went something like this:

Caller: "Is there any sex or nudity in the film?"

Hicks: "No, but there is quite a bit of violence and profanity."

Caller: "Well, that's all right. I just don't want my kids to see anybody naked."

The second went in a different direction:

Caller: "How violent is it?"

Hicks: "Well, it's very violent — and there's a fair amount of profanity."

Caller: "I don't care so much about the profanity, but I don't want my kids to see any really bloody, gory violence."

Similarly, I've had calls from people at various times who are more put off by profanity or by any number of other potentially offensive elements, such as drug abuse or lack of moral or ethical values, in various films. What this points out, of course, is that personal tastes are very personal indeed. Even people who have the same basic set of standards may differ widely on what they find most offensive in entertainment.

Here's the typical scenario, something I hear from people all the time: A friend at the office recommends a particular movie. You go to see it and, for the most part, enjoy it. But you find one or two moments offensive. Later, when you tell your friend about the offending scene(s), he at first looks surprised, then remembers and expresses chagrin. He simply forgot about the moment in the context of a film that he enjoyed overall. And he may not have been as offended as you were by that scene.

This isn't meant to indict the friend. This sort of thing happens to everyone at one time or another. It's simply a hazard of taking in modern entertainment.

Which brings us to this book.

First, let me state clearly that I do not intend this volume to be an all-inclusive collection of movie reviews. If you want a capsulized list of every movie available on video or something that tries to list every film that might turn up on television, look elsewhere. There are plenty of comprehensive books on those subjects already on the market. Nor do I mean this to be a cerebral book of analysis. There probably isn't a movie genre, celebrated filmmaker, or aspect of filmmaking that has not already been picked apart by writers. Further, I do not intend this book to be for movie buffs, although I hope they might find some enjoyment here.

I have written this book for average moviegoers who, when they take in a movie or rent a video, feel a bit overwhelmed by the scads of titles playing in local theaters or lining the video store shelves. They want to be more knowledgeable about movies, and most important, they want something they can watch by themselves or with their family without embarrassment or worry. For the most part, I simply attempt to answer some of the questions I am most often asked in my job as a movie critic. Among them are these:

What are the qualifications of a movie critic?

How does the rating system work?

Who can we write to when we have a complaint about a movie?

Why are so many children's films so vulgar?

Why don't they make movies like they used to?

Where can we get the edited versions of movies shown on airplanes?

Why do so many critics hate computer coloring and love letterboxing?

What do those credits at the end of the movie mean — like gaffer *and* dolly grip?

What are some movies we can rent that won't offend us — especially for Halloween?

Some of these things are more subjective than others, but I've addressed them from the perspective of both a movie critic and a parent. And the bulk of the book consists of an extensive list of recommended videos families can watch together.

Despite complaints registered here about the motion picture industry and its obvious lax attitude toward movies made for or sold to children, I have, on the whole, tried to take a positive approach. Rather than just whine about how so many movies are terrible or how even the good ones seem to always contain something offensive, I've tried to accentuate the positive — in particular with video recommendations. I've tried to have some fun with all this, because going to movies and watching videos should be fun.

When you get to the video recommendations, you'll discover many that are personal favorites of mine, movies I can watch repeatedly and still enjoy — especially when introducing them to my children for the first time. However, there are also movies that I might not be inclined to choose but that other people have indicated to me they enjoy. I hope this provides a well-rounded picture of what's out there to rent or purchase for families.

I also want to emphasize that these video recommendations are mine and mine alone. They do not necessarily represent the views of the publisher or of anyone else associated with this book. And, as I often say in my *Deseret News* columns, your comments are both welcome and encouraged.

■ ■

ON BEING A MOVIE CRITIC

■ ■ ■

MUSINGS ON THE PROCESS

■ ■

Once, while I was pumping gas at the local self-serve minimart, a fellow leaped over the island as he ran toward me and demanded to know why I had given a negative review to a movie he said was the best he'd seen in ten years. Another time, a woman in a grocery store stared at me for the longest time while we stood in line at the checkstand. Finally, she said, "You seem like a nice person. How come you don't like Kevin Costner?" And after a screening, as people came up to ask my opinion of the film we had just seen, a woman charged toward me, interrupted the conversation, and said, with no small amount of vitriol in her voice, "I loved this movie no matter what you say. And that's why I never listen to you. If you like a movie, I know I'll hate it. And if you don't like it, I know I'll love it."

Being a movie critic is a very strange job.

On the surface, it sounds like nothing but fun. Picture this conversation between editor and reporter at a great metropolitan daily:

"OK, Hicks. Enough of this hard-news reporting stuff. You've had all the front-page stories you're going to get. From now on we want you to go sit in darkened theaters and watch movies all day."

"Sure, boss. Sounds great. Where do I sign up?"

"Right on the dotted line. Oh, yeah, and there's one other teensy-weensy little thing. You'll have to write down your opinions of each movie you see for all the world to see. In print. No way to back down." (Then he starts to laugh.)

"Well, OK. No problem. I can handle it."

Right.

After a while, you discover there are only so many words in the dictionary to describe good, bad, or indifferent. And to make matters worse, everyone in the world and his cousin have opinions about each movie, and all of their opinions differ from yours. Plus every single person wants to know what makes yours so special.

There are also certain movies that I know will get me in trouble, even before I've seen them. Quirky, offbeat films, as disparate as *The Adventures of Buckaroo Banzai, Raising Arizona,* and *Edward Scissorhands,* will always garner phone calls or letters complaining that my endorsement was misleading. Not to mention "art" films — especially foreign films. Anything with subtitles.

On the other hand, negative or lukewarm reviews of *Wayne's World* or *Hook* or *Home Alone* will have people complaining that I didn't like them enough.

It's also sobering to realize that whenever I'm with a group of people — no matter how large — odds are I'm the only one who has seen all eight *Friday the 13th* movies, all five *Police Academy* films, and all the inferior clones to those and other popular pictures. In fact, quite often I'm the only person who has seen even one of them.

But I'm really not complaining. Honest. Because even after sitting through all those turkeys, and occasionally wondering if I shouldn't chase the next ambulance that comes along so I can win back my old city desk position, a reminder of what's so great about this job comes along.

One *Field of Dreams* can make me forget all the Freddy Krueger films. Seeing a *Henry V* or a *Beauty and the Beast*

6

or a *Howards End* or *A River Runs through It* makes me remember how much fun it is to go to the movies, to be able to kick back and thrill at periods and places, adventures and characters that I will never be able to personally experience or meet.

And small pleasures like *China Cry* or *Pastime* or *Alan & Naomi* remind me of what I like best about this job — the possibility of steering moviegoers toward some wonderful little picture that might otherwise be overlooked, the ones that are invariably trampled beneath the rush of commercial hits like *Teenage Mutant Ninja Turtles* and *Batman* sequels

It's my job to offer personal opinions, to try to assist readers in making up their own minds about whether they want to see a certain movie. I offer descriptive information in general and a subjective viewpoint in particular, but that doesn't mean my opinion is necessarily more valid than yours. As a movie critic for a daily newspaper, and for the purposes of this book, I see myself as something of a consumer reporter, helping moviegoers and video watchers decide what they want to spend their hard-earned entertainment bucks on.

You may decide to see a movie I hate or you may decide to skip a movie I love, but either way I hope the information here will help you make that decision. Besides, in the end, a review is really just an explanation of how the movie affected the reviewer personally.

One of the things I'll probably never get used to is how upset people get when they disagree with a review. And it just seems to irritate them more when they call to express their disagreement and I refuse to argue about it. I enjoy hearing how others feel about particular movies — what they liked or disliked about them and why — especially when their viewpoint differs from mine. I think it's healthy to disagree — and even healthier to agree to disagree.

In March of 1988, when I was interviewing Alan Alda in Denver for his movie *A New Life,* he suddenly turned

7

it around and began asking me about my job. Toward the end of our half hour together, he seemed genuinely curious about the process of reviewing movies, and he asked how many films I had seen the day before. I told him the truth — three. If that wasn't enough, I also went to an early movie the day of our interview, before catching a plane to Denver.

Alda wanted to know how, with all those movies bouncing around in my head, I could give his film — or the others I'd seen — the necessary attention to analyze them. It was a fair question, but the answer seems simplistic: I just do my best to evaluate each film on its own terms. Working for a daily newspaper that doesn't have the luxury (i.e., budget) of having two or three people cover Hollywood (as is the case with some of the large metropolitan dailies around the country), I see every movie that comes through town — roughly 250 a year. I take notes and try to be fair.

But we're talking about personal taste, after all, and that was the aspect Alda seemed most concerned about — whether the critic's personal taste doesn't get in the way, considering how diverse the movies are. There's no question that one has to shift gears in order to see a violent thriller in the morning, a sensitive character study in the afternoon, and a mid-life crisis comedy in the evening. It is possible, though, to set personal prejudices aside and shut down worldly concerns to just concentrate on the film.

But perhaps of primary importance is that the critic appreciates the medium he covers. We've all read reviews by TV critics who obviously disdain television, theater critics who don't seem to like stage plays, and movie critics who feel that a decent film hasn't been made since 1939. When I am asked what qualifies me for this job, I immediately respond that I love movies. I've always loved movies. To me, that's the bottom line.

Movies can be entertaining, artistic, or trashy. But regardless of the achievements of individual films, the medium as a whole has great possibilities, and those possibilities are what the critic should strive to encourage.

Yes, the rewards of being a critic are many. And I won't forget again. I love the job. And I'm grateful to the chuckling editor who placed me there.

Now where's that mail I was going to go through? Let's see . . .

Dear Mr. Hicks,

What kind of idiot would give four stars to . . .

■ ■

RATING THE RATINGS

■■■

ALPHABET SOUP

■ ■

Question: So what is it, really, that separates a G from a PG, a PG from a PG-13, and a PG-13 from an R, in terms of movie ratings?

Answer: Not much.

The wire-thin line of separation seems to be getting thinner and thinner as movie audiences, especially parents, become more and more puzzled over how to determine which movies will be the least offensive—and not just for children, but often for themselves.

I have a friend named Ray Boren who occasionally asks me if certain movies are "Mommy-rated." What he means by this is, can he safely take his mother to a particular movie, one that won't offend her with its excesses?

In this case, it's not enough just to know that a movie is rated PG, or even that the rating is due to some violence or sex or profanity. Ray wants to know how much. You see, his mother can take a swear word or two. And she won't flinch at a couple of characters coming to blows. Even an implied bedroom tryst, if it's done tastefully, can be acceptable. But if there's a plethora of profanity or buckets of blood or lingering nudity or too much camera time spent focused on a couple thrashing about under the sheets, Ray knows his mother won't be able to enjoy the movie — no matter how well-intentioned the film may be. His mother will simply be too busy squirming uncomfortably in her theater seat.

Ultimately, the question becomes, does what the movie has to say overpower its excesses, or do the excesses overpower what the movie has to say?

Too often, it is the latter.

So, Ray takes his mother to movies like *Father of the Bride, Field of Dreams,* and *Driving Miss Daisy* — all highly successful films that probably brought out much of the older audience that normally stays home — because it's safe to say those movies were "Mommy-rated."

But extra information is needed to make that determination. It isn't enough to know that these movies are rated PG. And the PG-13 and R labels aren't enough either. Too often the films within those ratings are too disparate in terms of the excesses they display on the screen.

For example, take *Housesitter* and *The Cutting Edge,* two PG-rated movies that contain raunchy sexual elements. Or the alleged family movie *A Far Off Place,* which is extremely violent. Those films carry the same rating as such innocuous children's fare as *Honey, I Blew Up the Kid* and *Beethoven.* Then there is the PG-13 category, which contains movies that look like PGs and movies that look like Rs: films as inoffensive as, say, *Awakenings* or *China Cry,* but also films that are much harsher, such as *Robin Hood: Prince of Thieves, Batman Returns,* and *Sommersby.* Similarly, in the R-rated category, there are films as soft as *Class Action* or *Let Him Have It* and films as rough as *The Silence of the Lambs* or *Basic Instinct.*

It's a conundrum, one that is not easily sorted out. In the end, the conscientious parent (or, in Ray's case, the conscientious child) needs more information than the rating alone supplies. Hence, this discussion, which I hope may help you gain a better understanding of how movie ratings work and why they cannot be taken at face value.

A BRIEF HISTORY

The movie rating system is our modern answer to the old Hays Code, which dictated what Hollywood could and could not display in movies during the 1930s, '40s, '50s, and, to a lesser extent, the '60s.

That code, named after Will H. Hays, then president of the Motion Picture Producers and Distributors of America, was a form of self-imposed censorship adopted by the Hollywood movie studios in 1930, revised with enforcement rules in 1934. The guiding principle was that no movie should sway the sympathy of the audience toward "the side of crime, wrongdoing, evil, or sin." But there were also specific bans against ridiculing the law, showing bedroom scenes that were not "governed by good taste and delicacy," and saying words and phrases from a long list that included such no-no's as "alley cat," "tart," and "pansy."

Today, of course, given our more permissive society, and seeing the extremely violent and raunchy movies readily available for public consumption, it seems that *anything goes*.

Our substitution for the Hays restrictions is the perennial G, PG, PG-13, R, and NC-17. But the Hays Code was an institution for more than thirty years, until the Classification and Rating Administration (CARA) was established in 1968 — and the ratings have been the subject of controversy ever since.

Under the auspices of Jack Valenti, who has been president of the Motion Picture Association of America (MPAA) since 1966, the ratings were designed for parents, to help them guide their children's moviegoing habits. The idea was that because movies in the '60s were becoming more and more explicit in terms of content, something had to be done to head off government censorship as the cries of parents became louder.

Originally the ratings were G, M, R, and X. But the M (for "mature") almost immediately became GP ("general audiences, with parental discretion advised"), and eventually the current PG. Today, the ratings are defined by the MPAA, this way:

—G. *General Audiences;* any age admitted. Nothing that would offend parents for viewing by children.

—PG. *Parental Guidance Suggested;* some material may not be suitable for children. Parents urged to give "parental guidance." May contain some material parents might not like for their young children.

—PG-13. *Parents Strongly Cautioned;* some material may be inappropriate for children under thirteen. Parents are urged to be cautious. Some material may be inappropriate for preteenagers.

—R. *Restricted;* under seventeen requires accompanying parent or adult guardian. Contains some adult material. Parents are urged to learn more about the film before taking their young children with them.

—NC-17. *No Children under 17 Admitted;* patently adult. Children are not admitted.

BUT WHAT DO THEY MEAN?

To put it more specifically:

—G-rated films contain no offensive material, specifically no profanity (although sometimes "damn" or "hell" might be allowed), no graphic violence (save slapstick), no sex, no nudity, no drug abuse, and so on. The truth is, however, that very few G-rated movies are made these days. It's an arena that is almost exclusively populated by animated films, though an occasional live-action children's film will get a G.

—PG-rated films might contain violence, profanity, sex, nudity, or other potentially offensive material, but the treatment is thought to be relatively tame or subtle. Still, it's a difficult category for parents, since movies specifically aimed at children, such as *Home Alone, Beethoven, The Mighty Ducks,* and *Honey, I Blew Up the Kid* all carry PGs, as do more adult films like *Housesitter, The Babe, A River Runs through It,* and *A League of Their Own.*

— PG-13 is a category created in 1984 after cries of outrage from parents who felt that *Indiana Jones and the Temple of Doom* and *Gremlins* (and, earlier, *Poltergeist*) were far too strong for their PG ratings. It is sometimes called "the Spielberg rating," since those movies were Steven Spielberg productions and he was influential in the MPAA's decision to come up with a rating between PG and R. Spielberg at the time described the movies as "too strong for a PG rating, but they aren't really R-rated movies either." The unfortunate result is that movies receiving PG-13 ratings today may be as tame as *Awakenings* or as harsh as *Batman Returns.*

— The R rating can be the roughest, of course, though there are exceptions. A few movies, such as *Glory, Ordinary People, The Verdict, A Few Good Men,* and *Class Action* don't really deserve to be labeled with this restrictive rating. But the fact is that most R-rated movies carry the rating because they do deserve it. They simply cross too far over the line. But when you get right down to it, the difference between an R-rated movie and a PG-rated movie is really very simple — the R-rated movie shows more, gets more explicit or graphic, the camera lingers longer, the amount of profanity is greater, and the drug abuse is more specific. And the roughest movies, such as *Total Recall, Reservoir Dogs, Body of Evidence,* and *Basic Instinct* are so rough that even the most liberal critics express surprise that they managed to be rated R when NC-17 seemed to be more appropriate.

— NC-17, of course, replaced the X rating in 1990. The G, PG, PG-13, and R rating symbols were trademarked by the MPAA, but the X was not. As a result, the X became a symbol for pornography, and it was often self-applied, without the movie ever going before CARA. The idea of the NC-17 category, of course, is to have a rating for movies that are strictly for adults — one that will not allow anyone under seventeen to be admitted. Certainly, one would think that *Total Recall* and *Basic Instinct* are adults-only movies, but the studios don't want to release NC-17 films for fear that theaters won't play them and audiences won't go to them—at least not in large enough numbers to make them huge hits. So, these films are nominally edited to qualify for R ratings. And the result is that certain movies push the limits of taste as far as possible and that more and more graphic material shows up in movies that carry R ratings. To quote Jack Mathews of *Newsday* in his review of *Basic Instinct:* "If this isn't an NC-17 movie . . . that adults-only category simply does not exist."

HOW THE SYSTEM WORKS

The CARA board is composed of eleven people hired from outside the movie industry. They must be parents, but there is no other qualification required. Their job is to represent American parents and apply the rating they feel most parents would find suitable. They are anonymous, their identities being kept secret so they cannot be influenced by moviemakers, and each serves up to two years on the board.

The result, of course, is that the board's membership experiences a fairly constant turnover. And on any given day, six or eight or nine people may be watching a particular movie instead of the full eleven, so the balance of power can shift from conservative to liberal at any given time.

Ideally, the ratings have no bearing on a film's quality. Whether they are looking at a documentary on the Holocaust or a teen sex comedy or a cartoon, CARA board members are to focus on the film's content, not on its quality. There is also an appeals board for those filmmakers who feel that the rating is unjustified. If a film gets an R, but the producer wants a PG, he can appeal to a twenty-one-member board comprised of industry insiders.

With regard to enforcement, that is, keeping fifteen-year-olds out of movies rated R or NC-17, we must remember that this is a voluntary system. There is no law that says movie theaters or video rental stores must comply. Most do their best to keep the system in check, but we all have our horror stories about kids seeing movies that their parents would rather they didn't. In those instances, all parents can do is complain. But the louder the complaint, the more likely it is that the theater owner or video dealer will be more careful next time.

MPAA president Jack Valenti estimates that 75 percent of parents with children under eighteen find the ratings "very useful" to "fairly useful" in helping them make decisions about their children's moviegoing habits. Parents I talk to would probably not give it such a high success ratio.

LOOKING AT THE NUMBERS

From its inception in 1968, CARA has rated nearly ten thousand movies. Half of those received R ratings, 30 percent received PG ratings, and the balance was split between the G, PG-13, and NC-17/X ratings. Yet if you look at the top one hundred money-making movies of all time, only twenty-six are rated R. Only thirteen of the top fifty movies are rated R. And there are no R-rated movies among the top ten biggest hits of all time. If it follows that the top money-making movies are the most popular movies, R-rated movies would seem to be much less popular with the moviegoing public at large than those rated PG and PG-13.

But Hollywood has never been able to get the message. When *E.T. The Extra-Terrestrial* became the biggest money-maker of all time in 1982, the movers and shakers didn't say, "Let's make more movies with heart and depth and humor and excitement, movies that will appeal to children and adults, that families can see together." Instead, they said, "Let's make more movies about little ugly aliens being befriended by children." And that's what we got for the next ten years.

CONCLUSIONS

While the rating system leaves much to be desired, it is certainly not without value. It's fairly obvious, after all, that a movie that carries an R rating is likely to be much more objectionable than a movie that carries a PG. So steering your young ones away from *Lethal Weapon 3* and toward *Honey, I Blew Up the Kid* is made easier for the parent who only glances at the movie pages.

But it does get fuzzy when you start looking at PG-rated movies that are more adult in nature or just about any PG-13–rated movies. If we conclude that all R-rated movies are problematic, we should not feel conversely that all films rated PG or PG-13 are perfectly OK. Some parents don't want their fourteen-year-olds exposed to nudity or sexual content, despite the PG-13 warning, while others may not want their children watching graphic violence or gunplay, even if the CARA board says it's OK for kids thirteen and older.

In short, it takes more than the MPAA's trademarked letters on the movie posters to determine whether the film will meet with your personal standards. The only way to be 100 percent sure is to see the movie yourself. Second to that is reading reviews or background stories, watching commercials, and scanning advertisements to help make a decision. But even that may be unintentionally misleading.

The rating board itself sometimes has trouble when it comes to getting specific. Though the board does now offer explanations for why it rates movies PG, PG-13, R, and NC-17, semantics tend to blur the meaning. For example, the word "sexuality" and the phrase "scenes of sexuality" are frequently used, but do they mean there is graphic sex or merely innuendo? And is there nudity involved, and if so, is it extensive or fleeting? And when the board says a movie is rated R for "some language" or "language," is that Hollywood's favorite cussword being spoken approximately once a sentence or a lot of other profanity, including deity being used in epithets?

Violence is apparently the most difficult area for board members, however, since R-rated descriptions include "war violence," "horror violence," "martial arts violence," "domestic violence," "monster violence," and so on. Occasionally the board will even go out on a limb with a phrase like "strong graphic violence" or "violence and gore." If the board itself has this much trouble coming up with succinct descriptions, imagine the dilemma critics have as they try to summarize "objectionable content" in reviews.

If you would like to write to the rating board, whether to complain, praise, or offer a suggestion, direct your letters to one of the three addresses listed below, offices of the Motion Picture Association of America (Jack Valenti is president of the MPAA, and Richard D. Heffner is chairman of the board of CARA):

14144 Ventura Boulevard
Sherman Oaks, California 91423

1133 Avenue of the Americas
New York, New York 10036

1600 Eye Street, N.W.
Washington, D.C. 20006

■ ■

LETTING KIDS REMAIN KIDS
■■■

AT LEAST THROUGH CHILDHOOD

■ ■

In February of 1991 the *Deseret News* sponsored a preview screening of *King Ralph,* a PG-rated comedy from Universal Pictures. Such previews are set up blind, of course — we don't see the movie in advance of the screening we sponsor. We just cross our fingers and hope for the best.

My children, the youngest being eight at the time, saw the *King Ralph* commercials on TV, which showed John Goodman in silly slapstick situations, and they were anxious to see the film. So I called Universal and asked if this was a family film or if I'd wish I had left my children home. I was assured there was nothing offensive and, yes, it was a family film. Well, even movie critics can be naïve. I took my kids to the screening, and you can imagine my chagrin when Goodman goes into a London strip joint and a woman disrobes directly in front of him (thankfully, with her back to us). And there were plenty of other vulgar moments that were equally distressing to a parent with young children. The upshot is that it provided some lively conversation between my children and myself on the way home.

This is hardly an isolated situation. The level of violence in *Kindergarten Cop* (rated PG-13), *Robin Hood: Prince of*

Thieves (PG-13), *Toys* (PG-13), *The Rocketeer* (PG), and *A Far Off Place* (PG); the continuous stream of vulgarity in *Drop Dead Fred* (PG-13) and *Problem Child 2* (PG-13); and the casual drug abuse in *Don't Tell Mom the Babysitter's Dead* (PG-13) — all movies that major studios sold directly to children with television advertising — are typical examples of how jaded the people who make movies have become.

Certainly, to some degree, audiences have also become jaded, but judging from the comments I hear from parents, most are still upset by the kinds of things their children are exposed to through the media — whether they are movies, television, music, magazines, even news. It's interesting how much more sensitive we are to such things when our children are sitting with us.

Maybe someone should establish a rule that people who make "family films" must have their own children sit next to them while they are filming. Is it asking too much to expect some semblance of sensitivity in pictures aimed at children? Well, maybe so.

CHILDISH ADULT FARE

Once upon a time, long, long ago, Hollywood seemed to know how to make movies for adults and movies for children — and sometimes movies that appealed to both adults and children. But today, movies are more often not suitable for either.

In *King Ralph,* for example, much of the humor is too childish for adults but a great deal of it is too vulgar for children. And *Kindergarten Cop* contains grotesque violence alternating with a sweet and funny plot about Arnold Schwarzenegger bonding with five-year-olds. (The TV ads emphasized the latter, of course.) *Look Who's Talking* (PG-13) and *Look Who's Talking Too* (PG-13) have an awful lot of vulgarity and sexual content, alternating with humor aimed at children. Similarly, much of *Three Men and a Baby* (PG), and to a lesser degree its sequel, *Three Men and a Little Lady* (PG), contain violence and an emphasis on sexual and vulgar humor that seem wildly inappropriate for young audiences. *Edward Scissorhands* (PG-13) has a moment of graphic violence at the film's climax that seems out of sync with the rest of the film, which is largely a gentle, sweet satire on modern suburbia and prejudice. And the *Home Alone* movies play out some questionable situations for impressionable eyes and ears.

In the antiwar satire *Toys,* Robin Williams plays a whimsical toymaker who is supposed to be a sheltered, completely innocent person. As if to offer a textbook case of how Hollywood is incapable of depicting innocence, however, *Toys* shows its lead character doing a number of things that seem counter to the very nature he is supposed to exemplify. He swears frequently. When he approaches a new female employee, he almost immediately makes a lewd, sexual proposition. And a bit later, they quickly wind up in her bed. *Toys* is a film that was sold directly to children through its television advertising, which emphasized the colorful, childlike toy factory, costumes, and set design and ignored the dark themes, violence, and sexual content, which are, of course, inappropriate for a very young audience.

Even the Walt Disney label is no longer a completely safe haven. Disney releases its more adult films through its Touchstone Pictures and Hollywood Pictures production arms, but the 1991 Walt Disney picture *White Fang* (rated PG), which was sold as a family film, contains profanity and a moment when a dead body pops out of a makeshift coffin and skids across an ice-covered lake, which might be something parents wouldn't want their kids to see. *The Rocketeer* (1991, PG) and *A Far Off Place* (1993, PG) also have far too much gunplay and killing for children's fare. And the latter has the additional lure of a Roger Rabbit cartoon.

All of this begs the question: *Did anyone go to these movies because of their violent or raunchy content?* And, *Would anyone have stayed away if the films had been toned down?* Absolutely not. Why, then, is there profanity in *White Fang* or nudity and vulgarity in *King Ralph* or all that violence in *Kindergarten Cop?*

AN APPEAL TO BE MORE APPEALING

On the surface, Hollywood filmmakers apparently throw these excesses into movies because they want the films to appeal to a broader audience. But instead of appealing to everyone, they often appeal to no one. If the moviegoers I hear from are any indication, even box office successes with offensive material send audience members out of the theater feeling they enjoyed the film *in spite* of those elements, not *because* of them.

But it's more than just the syndrome of cynical movies-by-committee. I think it's because these filmmakers have lost touch with, for lack of a better term, "middle America." Many of the people in Hollywood once lived outside Los Angeles or Manhattan and co-existed with ordinary people on a day-to-day basis. But once they became successful, most of them radically changed their life-styles to include chic dining spots, expensive parties, mingling with "beautiful people" and, often, drugs. So they find it hard to remember what life was like before.

As a result, we get a huge number of movies about high rollers, wheeler-dealers, wealth and power, artists, filmmakers, writers, and so on. Movies about common people the average moviegoer can identify with are becoming more and more scarce. And it seems a logical extension that these moviemakers have also forgotten what retaining some semblance of innocence during childhood means. The result is that filmmakers throw in sex, nudity, violence, and especially profanity in even the most child-oriented film fare.

If you question the filmmakers themselves on this subject, many will become defensive and say they include such material simply because children are exposed to it every day in one form or another—even in elementary school yards. To some degree that may be true. But if you talk to teachers—or even to the children themselves—they will tell you that when such offensive material is brought to the school yard, it has often come from a movie.

Besides, if children get this sort of garbage every day in the school yards, that seems like a reason not to give it to them in entertainment. No one has ever accused Hollywood of trying to take the higher road—but maybe it's about time moviemakers attempted just that.

■ ■

IS IT REALLY GETTING WORSE?

■ ■ ■

WHAT HAVE WE ACCEPTED?
WHERE ARE WE HEADED?

■ ■

There's no question that Hollywood has systematically lowered its standards over the past couple of decades, but it reached a new nadir with the box-office success of the hard R-rated *The Silence of the Lambs* — the fourth biggest money-maker of 1991 (crossing over the coveted $100 million benchmark). And with an Oscar coup that followed, the film has also been embraced by the Hollywood community as high art.

There was a time when gory, cannibal horror yarns were strictly fodder for the lower half of drive-in double bills. A movie like *Lambs,* no matter how well made, would never have been nominated for an Oscar. And if it were nominated, it would never have had a chance of winning. If there is a message here, it is simply that today anything goes, no matter how gruesome, graphic, or distasteful. And the more realistically it is portrayed, as opposed to the cartoon violence of something like *Terminator 2: Judgment Day,* the more respectable it becomes.

Of course, back in March of 1991, when *The Silence of the Lambs* was initially released, critics around the country were falling all over themselves praising director Jonathan

Demme for not making *The Silence of the Lambs* any more gory than he did. "Restraint" was the word most often used to describe Demme's film adapted from Thomas Harris's novel about an imprisoned cannibal serial killer and psychiatrist, and the way he helps a young, naïve female FBI trainee track down another serial killer.

But whether or not the film seems restrained probably depends on whether your own movie appetite leans more toward *Total Recall* or *Driving Miss Daisy*. Those who take in a regular diet of gory horror and/or action films, from the *Friday the 13th* series to Arnold Schwarzenegger's steady stream of violence-laden pictures, probably *did* feel Demme pulled back some. But those who do not regularly attend such movies no doubt felt assaulted. The truth is, *The Silence of the Lambs* is really little more than a gussied-up B-horror movie with an A-cast, a big budget, and a first-class director. But it is a B-horror movie nonetheless. In fact, much of its plotting and structure are right out of dozens of low-budget horror yarns that never broke out of the genre into mainstream film success.

The Texas Chainsaw Massacre is also about contemporary murderous cannibals — as are *Bloodthirsty Butchers, Cannibal Girls, Raw Meat, Motel Hell, C.H.U.D.,* and any number of other so-called "splatter" films. But do any of those sound like films you would likely take your spouse or friends to see? Probably not. But *The Silence of the Lambs* boasts very slick treatment, making the movie not only acceptable to audiences who would never dream of going to *The Texas Chainsaw Massacre,* but downright appealing. So much so that the film crossed over that important $100 million mark in its initial release, which happens only when at least some of the audience attends the movie more than once.

If that's not enough, *Lambs* went on to win the top five Oscars — for best picture, best actress, best actor, best adapted screenplay, and best direction, only the third movie in film history to cop those top five Oscars (the other two being *It Happened One Night* in 1934 and *One Flew Over the Cuckoo's Nest* in 1975).

But the question remains, does Demme show restraint in his direction of *The Silence of the Lambs?* In comparison with *A Nightmare on Elm Street* and its sequels, in comparison to *Total Recall* or Stephen King's *Sleepwalkers* or any number of other so-called "horror" or "action" thrillers, perhaps. But, with its depictions of cannibalism, bloody killings, human skins sewn together, and graphically displayed dead bodies, Demme has certainly thrown open the door for mainstream movies to be more gory than they have ever been before. One has to wonder where this will lead in the years to come. Especially in the work of filmmakers less skilled than Demme.

A FEW THINGS I WOULDN'T MIND NEVER SEEING AGAIN

The problem with movies, as opposed to other storytelling art forms, is that they are so literal. We see on an oversized screen as much as the film's director wants to show us. If, for example, he stops a scene with the bedroom door being shut, our imaginations fill in the rest. If, however, his camera follows the actors into the bedroom and details their, uh, actions further, our imaginations needn't hang around. It's not like reading a book or hearing a radio drama or even watching a play. What is visualized when watching a movie is entirely up to the movie director, not the moviegoer.

For many people who enjoy movies, but who do not enjoy tastelessness or embarrassment or simply being grossed out, it's hard to decide whether to attend a particular film despite its offensive content, or whether to avoid it despite its redeeming value. I take the optimistic approach. Once I've recorded the information necessary for a review, which includes the content likely to be responsible for the film's PG or PG-13 or R rating, I tend to forget it. When people call and ask about a certain film, often I have to go look up my own reviews. I may not be all that different from other moviegoers. I think most people tend to come away from good movies remembering the good parts. We put the bad parts away someplace where they can't bother us.

But some things are done so often in movies it's becoming harder and harder to ignore or forget them. In terms of what the audience tolerance level is for movies that, as they say in Hollywood, "push the envelope," it's different for everyone. For example, as far as I'm concerned, gore has worn out its welcome. Actually, I first wrote that in 1983, and look how far we've come since then. Just when you're sure movies can't possibly go any farther, someone in Hollywood feels the need to crank it up a notch. In horror movies, I prefer being scared through story development and characters who earn my sympathy to being grossed out by watching random teens mutilated and dismembered. But gore is far from the only offensive aspect of movies that has worn out its welcome where I'm concerned. Here are a few other things I wouldn't mind never seeing in movies again:

—Severed limbs. This is the kind of thing Arnold Schwarzenegger and Steven Seagal revel in, in movies like *Total Recall* and *Out for Justice.*

—Children in peril. The easiest, quickest way to get the audience to sympathize with the good guy and hate the bad guy is to have the villain threaten a youngster. *Lethal Weapon* and *The Last Boy Scout* both had an image I'm not fond of—someone holding a gun to a child's head. It even popped up in the children's film, *3 Ninjas.*

—Children swearing. When did it become vogue for youngsters, particularly preadolescents, to spew vile words, whether profanities or vulgar phrases? A decade ago the big joke in movies was a little old lady swearing. Now it's children.

—The Eddie Murphy/Bruce Willis word. This four-letter obscenity is not simply used by a character once or twice in anger anymore. It's become an integral part of the language in some films. It's even used as a syllable in the middle of other, more common words. Perhaps we need to organize a charity — *Please Give to the Thesaurus-for-a-Screenwriter Fund.*

—Obscene gestures. Whenever someone offers the most typical of these, using the middle finger, it's done with such flourish that you wonder if the filmmaker really believes that it's the first time it's ever been done in a movie.

—Flatulence and burping. Like obscene gestures, filmmakers who use these as comic devices seem to think they are original. It's the cheap-joke route for filmmakers who are humor-impaired.

—Nudity. Why do women continue to do nude scenes? It's obvious that men who make movies are exploiting actresses who disrobe in their films.

Say what you will about the old days — movies may have been less technically refined, less rooted in realism, and more fanciful. But they were also a lot more creative. Today, too many movies look too much alike, and usually in ways that are not flattering.

■ ■

AIRLINE CUTS

■ ■ ■

THOSE EDITED MOVIES YOU SEE ON PLANES

■ ■

My radio and TV partner Doug Wright saw *Mystic Pizza* on a long airline flight and enjoyed the romantic comedy so much that when he got home, he rented the movie to share it with his family. But as the film got going, he was surprised at the profanity and sexual content, which he did not remember from his initial viewing. "Did I fall asleep during those parts?" he asked himself. No, what he saw on his flight was an "airline cut," an alternate version of the film edited to tone down offensive content and eliminate profanity, in much the same way that movies are edited for commercial television showings.

Moviemakers may not realize it, or they are oblivious to it — or maybe they just don't care — but their movies could actually have a longer recycled shelf life without excessive profanity, violence, and other objectionable material. In fact, just making airline cuts available to the public could expand the life of a film. According to the airlines, people often leave a flight in which they've watched a cleaned-up version of a movie and ask where they can buy a copy. Why? Because they'd love to share *Rain Man* or *Beverly Hills Cop* or any number of other R-rated films with their families, but they don't want to expose them to the offensive elements those films contain.

At the moment, such edited versions are not available to the general public. There is a movement afoot, though, urging the studios to release them. And you can bet that if the studios felt confident that airline cuts would make money, they would release them.

Another hurdle is that airline cuts are often protested by the filmmakers. They feel their art has been tampered with when studios sanitize movies without their input — even with as small a change as a single profanity being deleted. Penny Marshall, director of such films as *Big, Awakenings,* and *A League of Their Own,* has said in interviews that when she saw the edited version of her PG-rated *Big* on an airline flight, she stood up and apologized to her fellow passengers because she felt the film had been "butchered." (She has also said that the single use of a harsh profanity in *Awakenings* was her idea and she considered it some kind of artistic triumph.) The edited versions of movies shown on network television also regularly come under fire, even though the filmmakers themselves are often called in to supervise the edits.

Of course, these special edits do not usurp the original film. If airline cuts were made available, anyone who wanted to rent or buy the original R-rated version of a movie could still always do so. On the other hand, those who would like to watch the film without its excesses would be able to.

In the meantime, since most modern movies show up on commercial television from time to time, you might want to consider getting blank tapes, setting up your VCR, recording the films you want when they show up on TV, and simply editing out the commercials. Then you could have your own cleaned-up version of any movie you want to add to your personal library.

For those who might wish to write to a movie studio, whether to request that airline cuts be made available on video or to ask for a favorite old movie to be released or just to praise or complain about a particular film, here are the major studios' addresses:

Columbia Pictures
10202 W. Washington
Culver City, CA 90222

MGM
1000 W. Washington Blvd.
Culver City, CA 90232

Miramax/Prestige
18 East 48th Street
Suite 1601
New York, NY 10017

New Line Cinemas/Fine Line Cinemas
757 Eighth Avenue
16th Floor
New York, NY 10018

Paramount Pictures
5555 Melrose Avenue
Los Angeles, CA 90038

The Samuel Goldwyn Company
10203 Santa Monica Blvd.
Suite 500
Los Angeles, CA 90067

Tri-Star Pictures
3400 Riverside Drive
Burbank, CA 91507

20th Century Fox
10201 W. Pico Blvd.
Los Angeles, CA 90035

Universal Pictures
100 Universal City
Universal City, CA 91608

Walt Disney Pictures/Hollywood Pictures/
Touchstone Pictures
500 South Buena Vista St.
Burbank, CA 91521

Warner Bros.
4000 Warner Blvd.
Burbank, CA 91522

GET A GRIP

•••

GIVING CREDIT WHERE CREDIT IS DUE

If you ever sit through the credits at the end of a film, which sometimes seem longer than the movie itself, you know that they always list a number of odd jobs. Of course, some films have jobs that are odder than others. *Indiana Jones and the Temple of Doom,* for example, had an "eel eater." In *Hook,* no less than 89 people were listed for "stunts" and some 160 for "special effects" — more than the entire crew on some less expensive films. And *Honey, I Blew Up the Kid* listed three "baby wranglers." Probably the funniest and longest-remembered oddball credit is this gem from the 1929 version of *The Taming of the Shrew:* "By William Shakespeare, with additional dialogue by Sam Taylor."

More recently, androgynous titles have replaced such traditional job titles as best boy, which is sometimes listed these days as "best person." But what the heck does a best boy . . . er, best person do?

Among the credits that appear on most every film are a few titles you may have wondered about. Is a gaffer one who keeps track of mistakes? Is the dolly grip someone who holds Dolly Parton on her mark? Is the negative cutter one who throws out insults? Is the boom operator the guy who lights the fuse for explosions?

Well, here's a brief glossary for future reference. You can amaze your acquaintances, astound your friends, and put your family to sleep by simply shouting out these definitions as the end credits appear on the screen:

Art director. The designer of the film's look, who works with the director and is usually in charge of both sets and costumes, though there are sometimes separate costume designers.

Best boy (. . . er, Best person). Assistant to the gaffer or grip (and sometimes an all-around gofer).

Boom operator. The person who handles the boom, a long-armed microphone that hangs above the actors, out of the camera's sight (or so the director hopes).

Camera operator. The person who actually operates the camera according to the cinematographer's instructions.

Casting director. The person who chooses supporting and minor acting roles (the director and producer select the stars). The casting director reviews resumes and photographs, looks at previous work by a performer, and holds auditions.

Cinematographer/Director of photography. The person who works with the director on lighting, composition, camera placement, movement, and related assignments.

Continuity. The matching of details in one day's shooting with subsequent shots that will eventually be edited together. This is usually the script supervisor's job. When it's done poorly, you might see an actor go through a door wearing a blue tie and enter the next room wearing a brown tie.

Director. The creative overseer who works with the actors, the cinematographer, set designer, and technicians in deciding how the film will be shot.

Dolby/THX Stereo. Two separate systems of recording sound that mute background noise and, when played back through quality systems, enhance the film with stereo sound effects and music.

Dolly grip/Dolly operator. The person in charge of the camera that is attached to a platform set on a track for moving shots.

Executive producer. Generally a title without a job. This is especially true for high-profile names, which are often listed solely to encourage financing. Sometimes the person might have input—especially if it's an additional title for the star or director.

Film editor. The person who, with assistants, edits or assembles the film footage into a narrative order that follows the script. Often the director and sometimes the producer are involved in this process.

Gaffer. Chief electrician.

Grip. The person in charge of props.

Matte work. Special effects achieved by placing one piece of film over another to give the illusion of background terrain, model ships in flight, or other elements in the scene.

Mixer. The sound editor who combines various audio elements for a film's final sound track.

Negative cutter. An assistant to the editor.

Producer. Also called the "line producer." This person is the money man or woman and overseer who may or may not be involved in the film's creativity. He keeps track of the overall project from start to finish, especially financial and administrative concerns. Associate producers, coproducers, etc., assist the line producer.

Second unit director. The director's assistant, who is in charge of the second unit. The second unit shoots special material, such as background locations or action sequences, usually without the stars.

Screenwriter(s). The person who writes the script, of course. When there is more than one screenwriter, the script has usually been rewritten—maybe many times. An exception is an ampersand connecting the names—Lowell Ganz & Babaloo Mandel, for example—which means they are a writing team. Often there are many more screenwriters involved than those whose names appear on the credits. When there are disagreements, the Writers Guild decides whose names are used and in what order. A "story by" credit is for the writer who came up with the concept or basic story or perhaps did the first draft script.

Sound effects. All sound in a film other than dialogue or music.

Steadicam. A camera first used in 1975 that permits hand-held filming with an image as steady as that provided by a camera with a permanent base. This camera is attached to a vest and distributes its weight on the cameraman's (or cameraperson's) hips.

CHAPTER
7

■ ■

COLORS AND LETTERBOXES
■■■

WHY CRITICS HATE COLORIZATION
AND LOVE LETTERBOXING

■ ■

Without a doubt, adding computerized colors to some old black-and-white movies on video has sold a few extra copies. And converting the general public to letter-boxing (as opposed to the pan-and-scan method used in most videos) is next to impossible. In these two areas, critics continue to be at odds with the public.

COLORIZATION VS. BLACK AND WHITE

Years ago, when my family was quite a bit younger, I wanted to share with my children the Laurel and Hardy short film *The Music Box*. The only version available at my local video store was computer-colored. But I rented it anyway, took it home, and put it in the VCR as the kids settled in to watch. After it started, I left the room for a moment. When I returned, the film was in black and white. "What happened?" I asked. My oldest son, Matthew, replied, "I turned down the color on the TV—Laurel and Hardy don't look right in color."

In my view, no black-and-white movie looks right in color.

The first computer-colored film I saw was *Topper*. The

second was the Laurel and Hardy comedy *Way Out West.* In both cases, computer coloring was a new technology and though it was intriguing, the color dropped out in places, and there was no vibrance — everything looked pallid and washed out.

Today, black-and-white movies that have been given color by computer are better-looking — but not by much. And, aside from a commercial perception that more young people will watch old movies that are in color, even bad color, there's no logical reason for doing it.

You've no doubt heard the critical arguments before: Movies shot in black and white were designed for that effect, and when color is added, especially to thrillers that rely heavily on shadow and light for effect, like *The Maltese Falcon,* the drama becomes as muted as the flesh tones. It is a mutilation of a work of art. And often the colors are simply wrong — the most famous example being the Frank Sinatra thriller *Suddenly,* in which "Ol' Blue Eyes" was given brown eyes! And, finally, it doesn't enhance the story or character or emotion of a black-and-white movie to give it color.

To quote Hal Roach, the veteran filmmaker whose many cinematic achievements were capped by the inspired teaming of Stan Laurel and Oliver Hardy: "Laurel and Hardy in color aren't any funnier."

PAN-AND-SCAN VS. LETTERBOXING

Letterboxing, that wide, rectangular picture made possible on TV's square screen by adding two broad black strips above and below the movie image, is appealing to those of us who want to get the full impact of what the filmmaker intended. Only letterboxing shows the entire scene on the screen.

In general, however, videos still use the pan-and-scan method, with the picture shifting from side to side to catch the most important action or dialogue in a given movie moment. The result is that we've all seen movies where one person is on one side of the screen and another person is on the other side—but only one of them is visible. Or worse, sometimes there's no shifting from the center of the image, and you can't see either of them, even though you hear dialogue.

Unfortunately, because watching letterboxed movies takes some adjustment of the human eye to get used to the wider, albeit smaller images on the screen, most video watchers don't want to bother. Certain movies, however, from *Lawrence of Arabia* to *West Side Story,* cry out for letterboxing. You simply miss too much in the traditional pan-and-scan form. For the time being, many more letterboxed films are available on laserdisc than videotape. Try a few. If you can get used to the format, you may prefer it to watching incomplete scenes in pan-and-scan.

CHAPTER
8

"HOW DO I GET MY KIDS TO WATCH BLACK-AND-WHITE MOVIES?"
###
A FEW SUGGESTIONS FOR STARTER KITS

Do you have trouble getting your kids to sit down and watch one of your favorite black-and-white classics? Do they start moaning when they notice the video you've chosen for the evening isn't in color?

In all probability, they've simply never seen a really good black-and-white film. Once they get into it, most people—regardless of their ages—tend to forget whether or not a movie is in color.

But the best way to break down this barrier is to start off with a good, rollicking comedy. Once they start laughing, kids usually forget to complain. And if they are real diehards about color, a good short film, one you can show before the color feature of their choice, might be the best way to start them off a bit more easily. Viewing Charlie Chaplin, Buster Keaton, Laurel and Hardy, or Abbott and Costello in brief doses before watching something more contemporary will ease them into such films. So, here are a few suggestions for short, black-and-white comedies that your kids might take to:

THE BALOONATIC/ONE WEEK. A pair of funny Buster Keaton silent

Joseph Francis Keaton, known as Buster Keaton.

shorts; in the first he's the pilot of a runaway hot-air balloon, while the second has him trying to put together a prefab house. (1923/1920, black and white, not rated.)

COUNTY HOSPITAL/SCRAM/TOWED IN THE HOLE/DIRTY WORK/GOING BYE-BYE. Many of Stan Laurel and Ollie Hardy's sound short films are available on various video collections. These five are among my favorites. (1926–35, black and white, not rated.)

THE GOLDEN AGE OF COMEDY. This compilation of silent comedy skits with a voice-over narration provides loads of amusing material, but most highly recommended is the hilarious montage of Laurel and Hardy bits, including a pie fight to end all pie fights. (1957, black and white, not rated.)

LAUREL AND HARDY'S LAUGHING 20'S. Collection of highlights from Stan and Ollie's best silent movie shorts, with some hilarious pantomime. (1965, black and white, not rated.)

THE MUSIC BOX. This Laurel and Hardy film won an Oscar as the best short film of 1932. It's one of their best. (Black and white, not rated.)

40

Bud Abbott (upper left) and Lou Costello (lower right).

THE NAUGHTY NINETIES. This feature stars Bud Abbott and Lou Costello, and though it's not their best film, about a third of the way into it the boys do their only recorded full-length version of the famous "Who's on First?" routine, a guaranteed laugh-getter. (1945, black and white, not rated.)

THE RINK/THE PAWNSHOP/THE IMMIGRANT/EASY STREET/THE FIRE-MAN. Several of Charlie Chaplin's short films are available in various combinations on various labels. Look for these titles on the various videos—they are the ones your kids will likely enjoy the most. All of them are chock-full of intricate slapstick comedy. (1916, black and white, not rated.)

STEAMBOAT BILL, JR. This is a Buster Keaton silent feature. In the final quarter of the film, you'll find a hysterically funny sequence involving a cyclone, where Keaton runs around trying to avoid falling trees and buildings. Your kids are guaranteed to laugh themselves silly. (1928, black and white, not rated.)

41

WHEN COMEDY WAS KING. A sequel to *The Golden Age of Comedy*, with wonderful silent movie clips, the highlight being Laurel and Hardy's *Big Business*, in which the boys sell Christmas trees door to door during the summer. (1960, black and white, not rated.)

■ ■

VIDEO RECOMMENDATIONS

■ ■ ■

A GUIDE TO FAMILY FLICKS

■ ■

You will no doubt observe some obvious omissions among the video recommendations that follow. Such popular fare as the *Indiana Jones* films, the *Batman* movies, and the *Teenage Mutant Ninja Turtles* flicks are not found here. That is not to suggest that movies you don't find here are not acceptable for youngsters, depending on their own sophistication and the parents' feelings about such material. Rather, they are omitted because they simply don't qualify universally as "family films," at least as I define that term.

In fact, you won't find any PG-13 or R-rated movies in these listings. And though I have tried to include as many modern, recent films as possible, the bulk of those listed here are older movies, made before the rating system came into being. Such films, of course, are not rated. All PG-rated movies include the reason for the rating, such as *Field of Dreams,* rated PG for profanity. From my perspective, the PG titles here have enough value to make it worth wading through a certain amount of objectionable material. You may disagree, of course, and in that case, I've tried to give you sufficient warning.

These are movies and programs I feel comfortable recommending for family viewing, and, with the exception of the Halloween section and perhaps a few specific films here and there, you should be able to sit down with your children or your mother or your clergyman or even your in-laws and watch these movies without fear of being embarrassed. At least, I hope so. And if I've missed the boat on that estimation, I'm sure someone out there will let me know. I look forward to hearing from you.

Another motivation here is to remind you of titles you may have forgotten about or, even better, introduce you to something you've never seen. In fact, some of these movies are so good, I envy those who will discover one of them for the first time.

Obviously, all of these titles are not available in every store, but if you call around, you should find what you're looking for. The following recommendations are listed in various categories, so you have some suggestions for types of movies as well as for holidays and special events. It's a fact that when the leaves start to change and October 31 is around the corner, the mood for a good, scary horror movie arises. And when the snow falls a little later in the year and department stores start putting up decorations, that's when a Christmas film seems like the perfect video for a chilly night. I hope that there are enough recommendations here to occupy your free evenings for a while.

OVERLOOKED GEMS

These are fairly recent movies you may have never heard of, little films, mostly low-budget independent productions (but some are from the Hollywood mainstream), that were largely overlooked in their initial theatrical releases. There are some real winners here, and all of them are worth a look.

ALAN & NAOMI. A young boy (Lukas Haas) growing up in 1944

Vanessa Zaoui in *Alan & Naomi*. ©1991 Leucadia Film Corporation. Used by permission.

Brooklyn is pushed by his parents to befriend a young French girl (Vanessa Zaoui) who has been traumatized by Nazi atrocities in her homeland. Heartfelt, touching, and thought-provoking. (1992, color, PG, violence, mild profanity.)

THE BALLAD OF GREGORIO CORTEZ. Gripping true story of a Mexican farmer who killed a sheriff through convoluted circumstances, then eluded six hundred Texas Rangers in a massive manhunt. Edward James Olmos is superb as the title character. (1985, color, PG, violence.)

CAREFUL, HE MIGHT HEAR YOU. Sensitive, touching Australian film about two sisters—one working-class and the other wealthy—in a Depression-era custody battle over their nephew, whose mother is dead; as told from the boy's point of view. Excellent performances. Wendy Hughes, Robyn Nevin, Nicholas Gledhill. (1983, color, PG, mild violence, a couple of profanities.)

END OF THE LINE. Light, Frank Capra-style comedy about two old railroaders who are put out to pasture, so they steal a train and head for Chicago to talk to the line's big boss. Wilford Brimley, Levon Helm, Mary Steenburgen, Kevin Bacon, Holly Hunter. (1987, color, PG, violence, profanity.)

HARRY'S WAR. Humorous farce in the Frank Capra tradition by writer-director Kieth Merrill, with hassled postal worker Edward Herrmann taking on the IRS. Geraldine Page. (1981, color, PG, violence.)

HEARTLAND. Finely crafted, moving true story of a widow (Conchata Ferrell) who becomes housekeeper to a taciturn Scotsman (Rip Torn) in 1910, striking up a tenuous relationship and eventually marrying him. Once in a while they do make them like they used to—and this is a prime example. (1980, color, PG, mild profanity.)

IRON AND SILK. Suprisingly good true story of an American's adventures in modern-day China, with Mark Salzman playing himself. (1990, color, PG, violence.)

JONI. Inspirational true story of Joni Eareckson (she plays herself), who broke her spine in a diving accident and rebuilt her life through hard work and religious faith, learning to paint and write using her teeth. (1980, color, G.)

LITTLE HEROES. Story of a poor girl and her dog in an uptight rural community. This is a pleasing mix of comedy and sentiment. (1991, color, G.)

LOVE LEADS THE WAY. True story from Disney about a blind man (Timothy Bottoms) who uses the first Seeing Eye dog. Well-acted by Bottoms and the rest of the cast, Eva Marie Saint, Arthur Hill, Susan Dey, Patricia Neal. Made for cable TV. (1984, color, G.)

MISS FIRECRACKER. Very nice, if somewhat uneven, comedy-drama of self-discovery as insecure Holly Hunter aspires to win the title pageant in her small Mississippi town. Mary Steenburgen, Tim Robbins, Alfre Woodard, Scott Glenn. (1989, color, PG, violence, profanity.)

NEWSIES. Original, live-action musical based on a strike in New York at the turn of the century. The raggedy kids who sell newspapers on street corners go up against the newspaper giant Joseph Pulitzer. The film is an unexpected delight. Nice songs (with music by *Aladdin/Beauty and the Beast/Little Mermaid* composer Alan Menken), athletic dancing, and fine performances by the young cast. (1992, color, PG, violence.)

Dance scene in 1899 New York from *Newsies*. ©Buena Vista Pictures Distribution. Used by permission.

NIGHT CROSSING. Well-made Disney film, the true story of a family escaping from East Berlin in a hot-air balloon, though it is surprisingly more thoughtful than exciting. John Hurt, Jane Alexander, Beau Bridges. (1981, color, PG, violence.)

PASTIME. An over-the-hill bush-league relief pitcher (William Russ) gives tips to a talented but shy young black rookie in the 1950s. Both are social outcasts and learn some of life's lessons together. Very nice little sleeper with excellent performances. (1991, color, PG, violence, profanity).

SILENCE OF THE NORTH. True story of a woman's survival in Canada's treacherous north country, with a very good central performance by Ellen Burstyn. Tom Skerritt. (1981, color, PG, violence, profanity.)

THE STONE BOY. Heartfelt, wrenching look at the human condition, a slow, deliberate story of the ways people react to tragedy. A young boy accidentally shoots and kills his older brother, and his parents are unable to help him deal with it. Excellent performances from the entire cast—Jason Presson, Robert Duvall, Glenn Close, Frederic Forrest, Wilford Brimley, Linda Hamilton. May be too disturbing for young children. (1984, color, PG, violence, a couple of profanities.)

47

TABLE FOR FIVE. This contemporary weeper has divorced Jon Voight trying to reenter his children's lives by taking them on a cruise to Europe. Better than might be expected, with excellent performances all around. Richard Crenna, Millie Perkins; look for Kevin Costner in a small role as a newlywed. (1983, color, PG, profanity.)

TAKE DOWN. A pompous English teacher (Edward Herrmann) is forced to coach the wrestling team of a small-town high school and seeks help from the young athlete (Lorenzo Lamas) he flunked. A winning combination of humor and drama from writer-director Kieth Merrill. (1978, color, PG, violence, one profanity.)

A TALENT FOR THE GAME. Edward James Olmos is a baseball scout who comes upon a surprisingly talented pitcher in this low-key, feel-good film. (1991, color, PG, profanity.)

TUCK EVERLASTING. A young girl discovers a strange family with a secret who lives in the woods near her rural home in this sweet-natured fantasy. Margaret Chamberlain, Paul Flessa, Fred Keller, James McGuire. (1980, color, G.)

TUCKER: THE MAN AND HIS DREAM. True story of Preston Tucker (Jeff Bridges), creator of an innovative car in the mid-'40s, who was forced out of business by powerful Detroit auto companies. Upbeat and old-fashioned, with something to say about American initiative; directed by Francis Ford Coppola. Martin Landau, Frederic Forrest, Mako. (1988, color, PG, profanity.)

THE WHALES OF AUGUST. Two elderly sisters, cheerful Lillian Gish and sour Bette Davis, squabble between visits from Ann Sothern, Vincent Price, and Harry Carey, Jr. A bit stiff and meandering, but an interesting character study. (1987, color, PG, profanity.)

WHO'S MINDING THE MINT? Goofball bunch of well-intentioned thieves break into the U.S. Mint to replace accidentally destroyed money in this underrated, very funny farce. Jim Hutton, Dorothy Provine, Milton Berle, Joey Bishop, Bob Denver, Walter Brennan. (1967, color, not rated.)

WHY SHOOT THE TEACHER? A new teacher (Bud Cort) in a small rural town during the Depression finds that it's an uphill battle to ingratiate himself to the stiff-necked townfolk. Good morality tale. (1980, color, PG, profanity.)

WILD HEARTS CAN'T BE BROKEN. Sentimental but enjoyable true story of a young orphan in the '30s who joins a carnival and becomes a stunt rider on a horse that dives into water from a forty-foot tower. Cliff Robertson. (1991, color, G.)

WITHOUT A CLUE. A funny slapstick take on Sherlock Holmes, with Ben Kingsley as Watson, the brains behind bumbling Michael Caine, an actor hired to play Holmes. (1988, color, PG, violence.)

COMODIES

SCREWBALL
...

BALL OF FIRE. Hilarious farce about a group of staid professors (led by Gary Cooper) whose work is upset by the presence of a burlesque dancer (Barbara Stanwyck). (1941, black and white, not rated.)

BRINGING UP BABY. This hilarious film is considered by most critics the pinnacle of screwball comedy, with eccentric paleontologist Cary Grant having his life turned upside down by daffy heiress Katharine Hepburn. Charlie Ruggles, May Robson, Barry Fitzgerald. (1938, black and white, not rated.)

HARVEY. James Stewart's best friend is his tall, imaginary white rabbit, "Harvey," in this reprisal of the comic stage hit, with Josephine Hull as the sister who wants to put him away. (1950, black and white, not rated.)

HOLIDAY. Engaging social comedy with Cary Grant and Katharine Hepburn as eccentric members of high society who were meant for each other—but he's engaged to her sister. Edward Everett Horton, Lew Ayres. (1938, black and white, not rated.)

LIBELED LADY. When his newspaper is sued for libel, the editor (Spencer Tracy) hires an old friend (William Powell) to compromise an heiress (Myrna Loy) and make the libel truth. Jean Harlow costars in this top-of-the-line farce. (1936, black and white, not rated.)

LOVE CRAZY. To win wife Myrna Loy back, William Powell pretends to be crazy in this goofy romantic comedy. Jack Carson. (1941, black and white, not rated.)

THE MATING GAME. Funny comic romance about a tax agent (Tony Randall) who becomes mixed up with a wacky rural family and reluctantly falls for a daughter (Debbie Reynolds). (1959, color, not rated.)

THE MORE THE MERRIER/WALK, DON'T RUN. A working girl is forced to share her apartment with two men, the older taking on the role of paternal matchmaker. The first film (with Jean Arthur, Charles Coburn, and Joel McCrea) is set during the World War II housing shortage in Washington, D.C.; the second (with Samantha Eggar, Cary Grant, and Jim Hutton) is set in Japan during the Tokyo Olympics. (1943, black and white, not rated/1966, color, not rated.)

MY FAVORITE WIFE. Very funny tale of a man about to be married when his first wife, thought dead years earlier in a plane crash, arrives on the scene. Cary Grant and Irene Dunne are in peak form here. (1940, black and white, not rated.)

OSCAR. Door-slamming farce with Sylvester Stallone playing it straight as a '30s gangster, surrounded by comic characters. Not great, but it does have some very funny moments. Don Ameche, Peter Riegert, Tim Curry, Eddie Bracken, Kirk Douglas. (1991, color, PG, mild violence, profanity, and vulgarity.)

THE PHILADELPHIA STORY. Classic high-society comedy with former husband Cary Grant crashing ex-wife Katharine Hepburn's wedding preparations, while reporter James Stewart falls for Hepburn himself. Stewart got his Oscar for this one. (1940, black and white, not rated.)

TWENTIETH CENTURY. Hyper screwball comedy at its zenith, with

John Barrymore as a Broadway producer who makes unknown Carole Lombard a star, loses her, and then tries to win her back during a train trip. Once they board the train and it shifts into high gear, this one's a riot. (1934, black and white, not rated.)

WHAT'S UP, DOC? Hysterical throwback to screwball comedies of the '30s (specifically *Bringing Up Baby*), with Barbra Streisand a goofy, overage college student who latches on to staid music professor Ryan O'Neal. (1972, color, G.)

DOMESTIC
...

BAREFOOT IN THE PARK. Very funny early Neil Simon comedy with Robert Redford (repeating his stage role) and Jane Fonda as newlyweds in a fifth-floor apartment in New York. (1967, color, not rated.)

CHRISTMAS IN JULY. Funny comedy of a clerk thinking he's won a slogan contest and going on a wild shopping spree, with Dick Powell in the lead and a cast of great character actors in support. (1940, black and white, not rated.)

THE EGG AND I. Funny rural comedy has farmer Fred MacMurray marrying city gal Claudette Colbert and introducing her to country life, along with a bevy of eccentric neighbors, led by Ma and Pa Kettle (Marjorie Main, Percy Kilbride). (1947, black and white, not rated.)

FATHER OF THE BRIDE. Whether you go for the more subtle style of Spencer Tracy in the original or the broader comedy of Steve Martin in the remake, you can't go wrong with this delightful comedy. (The original also boasts stunning Elizabeth Taylor as the bride; the second, Kimberly Williams.) (1950, black and white, not rated/1991, color, PG, one vulgar joke. The 1951 black-and-white comedy *Father's Little Dividend,* a sequel to the Tracy-Taylor film, is also good.)

FOLLOW ME, BOYS. Sweet tale of an ordinary Joe (Fred MacMurray) who relocates to a small town and starts a Boy Scout troop, winning the heart of a local girl (Vera Miles) along the way. (1966, color, not rated.)

51

HOME ALONE. Though marred by some vulgar exchanges early on, this exercise in cartoon violence with young Macaulay Culkin taking on comic burglars touched audiences and became one of the biggest money-makers of all time. Joe Pesci, Daniel Stern, Catherine O'Hara, John Candy. (1990, color, PG, violence, profanity; the 1992 sequel is more of the same.)

LIFE WITH FATHER. Funny, bright true story of a Victorian family, the strict father (William Powell) and more liberal mother (Irene Dunne). Based on the Broadway play. Elizabeth Taylor, Edmund Gwenn, ZaSu Pitts. (1947, color, not rated.)

THE LONG, LONG TRAILER. Broad slapstick farce with Lucy and then-husband Desi Arnaz playing newlyweds on their honeymoon in the title RV. Marjorie Main, Keenan Wynn. (1954, color, not rated.)

MR. BLANDINGS BUILDS HIS DREAM HOUSE. A forerunner of *The Money Pit,* this funny tale of a couple (Cary Grant, Myrna Loy) trying to get out of New York by building a home in the country is loaded with good humor and charm. (1948, black and white, not rated.)

MY GIRL. Funny, touching comedy-drama about a young girl (winning Anna Chlumsky) in a small town, circa 1972, who has an obsession with death and jealous feelings toward her mortician father's new girlfriend. Good message about dealing with death, but too rough for young children. Dan Aykroyd, Jamie Lee Curtis, Macaulay Culkin. (1992, color, PG, violence, profanity, vulgarity, dead bodies.)

PLEASE DON'T EAT THE DAISIES. In this domestic comedy, drama critic David Niven and wife Doris Day cope with a new house in the country and with their four children. (1960, color, not rated.)

THE THRILL OF IT ALL. Funny spoof of TV commercials, with Doris Day as an average housewife chosen to pitch products on the tube, much to the chagrin of husband James Garner. Arlene Francis, ZaSu Pitts. (1963, color, not rated.)

WITH SIX YOU GET EGGROLL. A widow (Doris Day) and widower

(Brian Keith) marry and blend their families in a rural home, with expected comic results. Barbara Hershey plays Keith's daughter; George Carlin, Pat Carroll. (1968, color, G.)

YOURS, MINE AND OURS. Widowed Henry Fonda and Lucille Ball try the dating game, then meet and marry, blending their family of eighteen children in this delightful comedy, based on a true story. Van Johnson, Tom Bosley. (1968, color, not rated.)

GHOSTS/SPIRITS
■■■

BLITHE SPIRIT. David Lean's wonderful adaptation of Noel Coward's comedy-fantasy about a widower (Rex Harrison) who remarries only to have his long-dead first wife come back to haunt him. Margaret Rutherford is a riot as a medium. (1945, color, not rated.)

FOREVER DARLING. Guardian angel James Mason tries to patch things up between troubled marrieds Lucille Ball and Desi Arnaz in this fantasy-comedy. (1956, color, not rated.)

THE GHOST AND MRS. MUIR. The ghost of a sea captain (Rex Harrison) romances a lonely widow (Gene Tierney) in this charming little comedy-fantasy. George Sanders, Edna Best, Natalie Wood. (1947, black and white, not rated.)

THE GHOST GOES WEST. When an English castle is moved, brick-by-brick, to the United States, the ghost that haunts it goes as well. Funny fantasy with Robert Donat, Eugene Pallette, Jean Parker, and Elsa Lanchester. (1936, black and white, not rated.)

HERE COMES MR. JORDAN. Very funny fantasy-comedy that later became Warren Beatty's *Heaven Can Wait.* Here, Robert Montgomery is a boxer who dies before his time and has to find a new body for his spirit. Evelyn Keyes, Claude Rains, Edward Everett Horton. (1941, black and white, not rated.)

THE HORN BLOWS AT MIDNIGHT. Very broad slapstick comedy fantasy with Benny as an angel sent to Earth to destroy it with a blast of Gabriel's horn. Pretty funny, despite Benny's jokes in later years that it ruined his movie career. Alexis Smith. (1945, black and white, not rated.)

TOPPER/TOPPER TAKES A TRIP/TOPPER RETURNS. Three delightful comedies about the hapless title character (Roland Young) who is hounded by ghosts. Cary Grant costars in the first film. (1938/1939/1941, black and white, not rated.)

BRITISH

...

CARLTON-BROWNE OF THE F.O. British foreign-office secretary Terry-Thomas is assigned to a forgotten British province and immediately sets about botching it up. Peter Sellers. (1959, black and white, not rated; also known as *The Man in a Cocked Hat.*)

I'M ALL RIGHT, JACK. Funny satire of labor-management relations, with bumbling Ian Carmichael inadvertently upsetting a crooked scheme. Peter Sellers, Margaret Rutherford, Richard Attenborough. (1959, black and white, not rated.)

KIND HEARTS AND CORONETS. In this hilarious dark comedy, Alec Guinness plays eight roles, all of them titled characters whom Dennis Price must eliminate in order to gain his inheritance. (1949, black and white, not rated.)

THE LADYKILLERS. Alec Guinness leads a mob of dumb hoods who use their little old landlady as an alibi in one of the best of the British caper farces. Peter Sellers, Herbert Lom. (1955, color, not rated.)

THE LAVENDER HILL MOB. Classic caper comedy with Alec Guinness as a mild-mannered bank clerk who comes up with a scheme for the perfect robbery. Stanley Holloway; young Audrey Hepburn has a bit part. (1951, black and white, not rated.)

THE MAN IN THE WHITE SUIT. Meek inventor Alec Guinness comes up with a fabric that won't wrinkle, tear, or get dirty. Naturally, the garment industry hates it. Very funny romp. (1951, black and white, not rated.)

THE MOUSE THAT ROARED. Hilarious satire has the Duchy of Grand Fenwick declaring war on the United States, hoping to lose and thereby gain foreign aid. But the plan backfires. Peter Sellers is terrific in three roles. (1959, color, not rated.)

THE SMALLEST SHOW ON EARTH. Very funny tale of a couple (Virginia McKenna and Bill Travers, later of *Born Free*) inheriting a run-down movie theater, along with equally run-down caretakers Peter Sellers, Margaret Rutherford, and Bernard Miles. (1957, black and white, not rated.)

TWO-WAY STRETCH. Peter Sellers plots with fellow inmates to escape from prison long enough to commit a robbery then return to their cells as the perfect alibi. Wilfrid Hyde-White, Lionel Jeffries. (1960, black and white, not rated.)

UP THE CREEK. Peter Sellers and Wilfrid Hyde-White topline this British navy spoof, with young lieutenant David Tomlinson receiving a run-down shore assignment. (1958, black and white, not rated.)

THE WRONG ARM OF THE LAW. Crooks masquerade as cops to take booty away from other crooks in this ingenious farce, with Peter Sellers, Lionel Jeffries, Nanette Newman. (1962, black and white, not rated.)

YOUR PAST IS SHOWING. Nasty Dennis Price blackmails a few too many people with threats of publishing their secrets. They get together and plot to rid themselves of him. Wickedly funny farce, with Peter Sellers and Terry-Thomas among Price's victims. (1957, black and white, not rated; also known as *The Naked Truth*.)

FRANK CAPRA
...

IT HAPPENED ONE NIGHT. This oscar-winning comedy has a cynical reporter (Clark Gable) following a runaway heiress (Claudette Colbert). Truly hilarious romance. (1934, black and white, not rated.)

MR. DEEDS GOES TO TOWN. Top-notch Frank Capra story of Longfellow Deeds (Gary Cooper), who inherits twenty million dollars, decides to give it away to the needy, and encounters all kinds of difficulty. Jean Arthur. (1936, black and white, not rated.)

MR. SMITH GOES TO WASHINGTON. Idealistic James Stewart becomes a senator and soon finds corruption everywhere he turns in this Frank Capra classic, with Jean Arthur as the cynical reporter who can't believe he's for real. Claude Rains, Edward Arnold. (1939, black and white, not rated.)

YOU CAN'T TAKE IT WITH YOU. Funny Frank Capra picture (based on the stage play) about a young woman (Jean Arthur) fearful of bringing her boyfriend (James Stewart) to meet her very eccentric family. Lionel Barrymore, Edward Arnold, Ann Miller. (1938, black and white, not rated.)

CHARLIE CHAPLIN
...

Charles Chaplin, who wrote and directed all of his greatest works, still made silent films into the mid-'30s, though sound had started taking over in the late '20s. Many Chaplin shorts are available in various collections; these are some of his best features:

CITY LIGHTS. Considered by critics internationally to be one of the greatest films of all time, Chaplin's classic tale of the "Little Tramp" struggling to earn money to anonymously pay for a blind flower girl's eye operation. Great mix of slapstick and sentiment with an unforgettable final scene. (1931, black and white, not rated.)

THE GOLD RUSH. Chaplin's classic story of his "Little Tramp" confronting dangers in the Yukon, including the classic boot supper. Chaplin wrote the music for reissue. (1925, black and white, not rated.)

THE KID. Alternately moving and hilarious film. The "Little Tramp" takes in and befriends an orphan (young Jackie Coogan), only to see him taken away by authorities. Coogan's realistic performance is still quite astonishing. (1921, black and white, not rated.)

MODERN TIMES. Chaplin at his best, struggling with the mechanized age and meeting up with gorgeous Paulette Goddard. His last silent film; Chaplin also wrote the music. (1936, black and white, not rated.)

BUSTER KEATON
...

Though Buster Keaton spent most of history in Chaplin's shadow, he is now recognized as a great athletic comic whose movies rival Chaplin's as art as well as laugh-getting entertainment. Keaton's shorts are also available in various collections; these are some of his best features:

THE CAMERAMAN. Keaton does tintypes, but to impress a young lady, he tries to become a newsreel photographer in this action comedy. (1928, black and white, not rated.)

COLLEGE. Gag-filled look at campus hijinks, with studious Keaton trying to excel at athletics for his girlfriend. Very funny silent farce. (1927, black and white, not rated.)

THE GENERAL. Considered the pinnacle of Keaton's career, a hilarious Civil War yarn in which he tries to retrieve his train from Union soldiers. (1927, black and white, not rated.)

OUR HOSPITALITY. First-rate Keaton, as he travels to Dixie to claim his family estate and falls for a member of a rival clan, with a suspenseful waterfall finale. (1923, black and white, not rated.)

SPITE MARRIAGE. Keaton's last silent film is quite funny, about a pants presser who sets his sights on a stage star. (1929, black and white, not rated.)

OTHERS
...

AROUND THE WORLD IN 80 DAYS. David Niven is Phineas Fogg in this adaptation of the Jules Verne tale, betting he can pull off the title challenge and meeting up with guest stars galore along the way. Cantinflas, Shirley MacLaine, Robert Newton, Marlene Dietrich, Frank Sinatra, Red Skelton, and others. Two tapes. (1956, color, not rated.)

BACK TO THE BEACH. Campy, off-the-wall lampoon of the old "Beach Party" pictures may appeal more to those who grew up in the '60s than modern-day teens, with Annette Funicello and Frankie Avalon gently spoofing themselves. Lots of TV guest stars. (1987, color, PG, a couple of profanities.)

BROTHER ORCHID. Edward G. Robinson hides out in a monastery in this comic twist on his famous gangster roles. Humphrey Bogart, Ann Sothern, Ralph Bellamy. (1940, black and white, not rated.)

THE COURT JESTER. Danny Kaye's best film, a riotous spoof of "Robin Hood" movies, complete with Basil Rathbone as the chief villain. Some terrific songs and great patter, including the "vessel with the pestle" routine. Angela Lansbury. (1956, color, not rated.)

DESIGNING WOMAN. Enjoyable comedy of sportswriter (Gregory Peck) and fashion designer (Lauren Bacall), whose marriage is one long string of clashes. (1957, color, not rated.)

ENCINO MAN. Goofy comedy about two high school kids finding a frozen caveman, thawing him out, and taking him to high school as an exchange student. Surprisingly clean-spirited. (1992, color, PG, violence, profanity, vulgarity.)

THE GLASS BOTTOM BOAT. Doris Day is a widowed writer mistaken for a spy in this merry romp of mistaken identities. Rod Taylor, Arthur Godfrey, Paul Lynde, Dom DeLuise, Dick Martin. (1966, color, not rated.)

THE GODS MUST BE CRAZY/THE GODS MUST BE CRAZY II. Funny slapstick farces about an African Bushman's encounters with "civilized" society. The first centers, of all things, on an empty Coke bottle. The second isn't quite up to the first, but it's still enjoyable. (1981/1989, color, PG, violence.)

THE GREAT RACE. Funny, if overlong, slapstick played like an old melodrama, with hero Tony Curtis in white and villain Jack Lemmon in black, racing from New York to Paris. Some very funny bits. Natalie Wood, Peter Falk, Keenan Wynn. (1965, color, not rated.)

HANS CHRISTIAN ANDERSEN. Danny Kaye, in the role with which he will always be most closely associated, as the spinner of children's fairy tales who falls in love with a ballerina. A bit too long, but good songs and colorful fantasy sequences help move it along. (1952, color, not rated.)

VIDEO RECOMMENDATIONS

THE HOT ROCK. Funny caper yarn with Robert Redford and a bungling crew setting up an elaborate robbery. George Segal, Zero Mostel. (1972, color, PG, violence, profanity.)

HOT STUFF. True story of Miami cops fencing stolen goods to capture burglary ring. Dom DeLuise stars (and directed); Suzanne Pleshette, Jerry Reed, Ossie Davis. (1979, color, PG, violence, profanity.)

I LOVE MELVIN. Cute comedy of Donald O'Connor romancing chorus girl Debbie Reynolds by pretending to be a photographer who can get her on the cover of *Look* magazine. (1953, color, not rated.)

THE IMPORTANCE OF BEING EARNEST. Very funny adaptation of Oscar Wilde's Victorian comedy of manners about the romantic complexities of two wealthy bachelors, performed by a superb cast—Michael Redgrave, Michael Denison, Edith Evans, Margaret Rutherford. (1952, color, not rated.)

THE IN-LAWS. Very funny tale of a mild-mannered dentist (Alan Arkin) whose life is turned upside down by his son's future father-in-law (Peter Falk), a zany spy. Arkin and Falk are a great team; Richard Libertini is funny as a kooky South American dictator. (1979, color, PG, violence, profanity.)

IT'S A MAD, MAD, MAD, MAD WORLD. Way too long and overblown, but with some very funny moments, this chase comedy is a lesson in the evils of greed, with ordinary folks (played by an all-star comic cast) racing to find a cache of cash. (1963, color, not rated.)

KISSES FOR MY PRESIDENT. Amusing if thin look at a woman who becomes president and at her befuddled husband who must deal with this. Polly Bergen and Fred MacMurray give it their all. Arlene Dahl, Eli Wallach. (1964, black and white, not rated.)

LILIES OF THE FIELD. Sidney Poitier won his Oscar as a handyman who helps nuns in Arizona build a chapel in this very enjoyable little film. (1963, black and white, not rated.)

MOVIE, MOVIE. Funny spoofs of old movies, primarily '30s-style musicals and boxing pictures, with George C. Scott, Eli Wallach,

59

Harry Hamlin, Barry Bostwick. (1979, color/black and white, PG, violence.)

NINOTCHKA. Funny satire of a humorless Russian agent (Greta Garbo) meeting up with a freewheeling American (Melvyn Douglas) in Paris and falling in love. (1939, black and white, not rated.)

THE PRINCESS AND THE PIRATE. Colorful spoof of pirate pictures, with Bob Hope as a shanghaied vaudevillian involved with a princess (Virginia Mayo). Walter Brennan, Walter Slezak, Victor McLaglen. (1944, color, not rated.)

QUARTERBACK PRINCESS. Helen Hunt stars as the title character in this true story about a homecoming queen who is also on the football team. Made for TV. (1983, color, not rated.)

THE RUSSIANS ARE COMING! THE RUSSIANS ARE COMING! Dated but enjoyable comedy about a Russian submarine accidentally landing off of New England, with good comic cast—Alan Arkin, Carl Reiner, Eva Marie Saint, Brian Keith, Jonathan Winters, Paul Ford, Theodore Bikel. (1966, color, not rated.)

THE SECRET LIFE OF WALTER MITTY. About halfway through, this comedy veers away from its James Thurber inspiration to become a routine spy farce, but it's still fun, with Danny Kaye perfectly cast in the title role. Boris Karloff, Virginia Mayo. (1947, color, not rated.)

THOSE MAGNIFICENT MEN IN THEIR FLYING MACHINES: OR, HOW I FLEW FROM LONDON TO PARIS IN 25 HOURS AND 11 MINUTES. Too long, but this comedy about the title race in 1910 is enjoyable. Red Skelton is funny in a prologue about early flight attempts. (1965, color, not rated.)

THE TROUBLE WITH ANGELS. Hayley Mills and June Harding are new students at a convent school, driving mother superior Rosalind Russell crazy in this comedy. (1966, color, not rated; the sequel, *Where Angels Go . . . Trouble Follows,* is not on video.)

VICE VERSA. Very funny tale of a father (Judge Reinhold) and son (Fred Savage) who find themselves inhabiting each other's bodies. (1988, color, PG, profanity, vulgarity.)

WHISTLING IN THE DARK/WHISTLING IN DIXIE. Red Skelton in the first two of a trilogy of mystery comedies as "The Fox," a radio detective. Ann Rutherford. (1941/1942, black and white, not rated.)

COMEDY TEAMS

There are no comedy teams these days, though comic stars like Bill Murray and Dan Aykroyd or Steve Martin and Rick Moranis do occasionally pair up for specific films. But there was a time when Laurel and Hardy, the Marx Brothers, Abbott and Costello, and Martin and Lewis were top box-office draws. And, though they had solo careers, Bob Hope and Bing Crosby also had big hits with their series of *Road* pictures, as did Spencer Tracy and Katharine Hepburn in their teamings. (Even such largely forgotten teams as Wheeler and Woolsey, the Ritz Brothers, and Olsen and Johnson were quite popular in their day.)

Until recently, each of these teams had only a limited number of films on video, but in the past few years that number has grown tremendously. I've tried to single out for recommendation five to ten of each team's best films:

MARX BROTHERS
...

Marxian Madness, as it is often called, is a unique blend of off-the-wall, satirical, and anachronistic humor with Groucho specializing in one-liners, Chico in puns, and Harpo in pantomime. There are no dreadful Marx Brothers movies, though the last two, *Love Happy* and *The Big Store,* come close. Groucho, Chico, Harpo, and Zeppo starred in five films in the early '30s, then Zeppo left the team, and Groucho, Chico, and Harpo starred together in eight more. All are on video.

The first two Marx films, *The Cocoanuts* and *Animal Crackers,* have many hilarious routines but are marred by

61

All four Marx brothers: (from left to right) Zeppo, Harpo, Chico, and Groucho.

early sound technology and static camera work, as well as silly musical interludes and dumb romantic subplots. *A Night at the Opera* is considered by most critics their best film; my personal favorite has always been *Duck Soup*.

A DAY AT THE RACES. Groucho is a horse doctor who pretends to be a physician when he's hired by a sanatorium. Some riotous bits. (1937, black and white, not rated.)

DUCK SOUP. Groucho rules a country in this zany antiwar film, with a wild climactic battle. (1933, black and white, not rated.)

HORSE FEATHERS. Groucho is a college president, and Chico and Harpo are spies, highlighted by a hilarious football finale. (1932, black and white, not rated.)

MONKEY BUSINESS. This is the Marx Brothers version of "Love Boat," with the boys stowing away on a cruise liner. (1931, black and white, not rated.)

A NIGHT AT THE OPERA. As the title indicates, Groucho, Chico, and Harpo wreak havoc at the opera with some of their most memorable routines. (1935, black and white, not rated.)

ABBOTT AND COSTELLO
...

Bud Abbott and Lou Costello specialized in knockabout slapstick. Many of the routines they made famous — including "Who's On First?" — were also done by other comedians during the burlesque and vaudeville eras, but none had the timing and comic chemistry that made Abbott and Costello beloved by moviegoers during the 1940s. Twenty-four of Abbott and Costello's thirty-six films are now available on video, including all of their best work. For the film that contains "Who's on First?" see chapter eight, "How Do I Get My Kids to Watch Black-and-White Movies?"

BUCK PRIVATES/BUCK PRIVATES COME HOME. Their first starring film is a military farce with some of their best routines. The Andrews Sisters provide some terrific songs. The sequel has more plot, with a wild race car finale. (1941/1947, black and white, not rated.)

HOLD THAT GHOST Very funny murder mystery comedy set in a "haunted house." Notable also for teaming Costello with the terrific comic female Joan Davis. (1941, black and white, not rated.)

IN THE NAVY/KEEP 'EM FLYING. Good pair of military comedies, follow-ups to *Buck Privates,* made when the boys were still young and at the peak of their form. (1941/1941, black and white, not rated.)

THE TIME OF THEIR LIVES. Unusual Abbott and Costello film has the boys playing roles apart from each other in the story of Revolutionary War ghosts (Costello and Marjorie Reynolds) trying to break the curse that holds them to a country estate. Very good. (1946, black and white, not rated.)

WHO DONE IT? Murder mystery comedy set in a radio station.

Laurel and Hardy. Full names: Arthur Stanley Jefferson, left, and Norvell Hardy, right.

Costello teams with the very funny comic actress Mary Wickes. (1942, black and white, not rated.)

LAUREL AND HARDY
•••

The rule of thumb with Stan Laurel and Oliver Hardy is to avoid the films they made post-1940, when they lost control over their material. Everything else is generally quite good, showing off their genial humor, wonderful comic timing, and the gentle, dumb friendship that endeared them to audiences well beyond their more than twenty years together.

Since Stan and Ollie made some seventy short films together, both silents and talkies, along with about twenty-five sound features, it's impossible to list all that are on video. For the best shorts, see chapter eight, "How Do I Get My Kids to Watch Black-and-White Movies?" Recommended below are some of their best features.

BLOCK-HEADS. Stan is discovered marching in a trench twenty years after World War I is over. Ollie brings him home. Big mistake. One of their funniest films. (1938, black and white, not rated.)

THE BOHEMIAN GIRL. Very funny operetta with good songs and some great bits, as when Stan tries to fill some wine bottles. (1936, black and white, not rated.)

OUR RELATIONS. Mistaken identities galore occur when Stan and Ollie's long-lost twin brothers suddenly appear in one of their regular haunts. (1936, black and white, not rated.)

PARDON US. In their first starring feature, the boys find themselves in prison. Some good bits, especially if you've ever seen an old *Big House* picture. (1931, black and white, not rated.)

SONS OF THE DESERT. Generally considered the best Laurel and Hardy film, this riotous yarn has them trying to escape their wives to attend a gathering of their fraternal order. (1933, black and white, not rated.)

WAY OUT WEST. Top-notch Western spoof has the boys trying to deliver a deed to a mine but getting waylaid. Good musical interludes this time out. (1937, black and white, not rated.)

TRACY AND HEPBURN
■■■

All nine of the battle-of-the-sexes comedies that Spencer Tracy and Katharine Hepburn made over a twenty-five-year period are now on video; these are the best:

ADAM'S RIB. As husband-and-wife lawyers on opposite sides of a murder case, Tracy and Hepburn have one of their finest outings. Judy Holliday, Tom Ewell, David Wayne. (1949, black and white, not rated.)

DESK SET. Tracy is an efficiency expert brought in by a TV network to improve Hepburn's research department with automation, but she surprises him with her own abilities. Funny romantic comedy, adapted from a stage play. Joan Blondell, Gig Young. (1957, color, not rated.)

GUESS WHO'S COMING TO DINNER. Warm, amusing look at liberal-

Spencer Tracy and Katharine Hepburn. Photograph used by permission of Turner Entertainment Company. All rights reserved.

thinking parents who are put to the test when their daughter brings home her fiancé, a black doctor. Great cast. Spencer Tracy, Katharine Hepburn, Sidney Poitier, and Katharine Houghton. (1967, color, not rated.)

PAT AND MIKE. Funny romantic comedy with Hepburn as Pat, a top golfer, and Tracy as Mike, who becomes her manager, as love starts to bloom. Aldo Ray, Jim Backus, Charles Bronson. (1952, black and white, not rated.)

STATE OF THE UNION. Frank Capra directed this one, with Tracy as a presidential candidate trying hard to hold on to his integrity and Hepburn as the estranged wife who comes back to help. Funny, witty, and surprisingly contemporary. Angela Lansbury, Van Johnson. (1948, black and white, not rated.)

WITHOUT LOVE. An eccentric scientist (Spencer Tracy) and a widow (Katharine Hepburn) marry for convenience and reluctantly fall in love in this light comedy. With Lucille Ball and Keenan Wynn. (1945, black and white, not rated.)

WOMAN OF THE YEAR. The first Tracy-Hepburn teaming is an ab-

66

Bob Hope and Dorothy Lamour made many movies together, including all seven *Road* pictures, costarring Bing Crosby (the first was made in 1940, the last in 1962).

solute gem, with sports reporter Tracy romancing and marrying politician Hepburn, with whom he has nothing in common. (1942, black and white, not rated.)

HOPE AND CROSBY
■■■

All seven of the Bob Hope and Bing Crosby *Road* movies, costarring Dorothy Lamour, are now on video — *Singapore, Zanzibar,* and *Morocco* were just recently released. These are the best.

ROAD TO BALI. The only color *Road* picture has Bob and Bing rescuing Dorothy from an evil princess in the colorful jungles of Bali. Some very funny bits, including a hysterical cameo by Humphrey Bogart. (1952, color, not rated.)

ROAD TO MOROCCO. Fast-paced entry in the series has Bing selling Bob to slave traders, then meeting up with princess Dorothy. Anthony Quinn lends support. (1942, black and white, not rated.)

ROAD TO RIO. Very funny entry has the boys trying to save Lamour, with no help from the zany Weire Brothers. Good songs, too, with the Andrews Sisters guesting. (1947, black and white, not rated.)

ROAD TO SINGAPORE. The first of the Hope-Crosby teamings has them as playboys trying to get away from women — until they meet Lamour. Anthony Quinn has a small role. (1940, black and white, not rated.)

ROAD TO UTOPIA. The most hilarious of the *Road* films has Bob and Bing in Alaska looking for a gold mine, though the plot is secondary to rapid-fire off-the-wall gags. (1945, black and white, not rated.)

MARTIN AND LEWIS
...

Though they both went on to popular solo careers, Dean Martin and Jerry Lewis began as a team, with Martin crooning a couple of tunes in between slow burns aimed at Lewis's manic antics. They have their individual devotees, but there are many fans who believe Martin and Lewis were at their best when they were a team. From 1949 through 1956, Martin and Lewis made sixteen films, though only seven are available on video — and unfortunately they do not include all the team's best films.

ARTISTS AND MODELS. Comic-book artist Martin gets inspiration from Lewis's wild dreams in this fanciful farce. Shirley MacLaine, Dorothy Malone, Anita Ekberg, Eva Gabor. (1955, color, not rated.)

AT WAR WITH THE ARMY. In their first starring film, Martin is a sergeant putting up with goofy private Lewis in this military farce. Polly Bergen. (1950, black and white, not rated.)

THE CADDY. Martin's a golf pro with Lewis as the bumbling title character. The film is framed by bits from their nightclub act. Martin sings his hit, "That's Amore." With Donna Reed. (1953, black and white, not rated.)

HOLLYWOOD OR BUST. Inventive farce has Lewis driving West to meet Anita Ekberg (playing herself) in Hollywood, picking up gambler Martin along the way. Martin and Lewis's last film together. (1956, color, not rated.)

JUMPING JACKS. This one, a service comedy with the boys as paratroopers, is one of their most enjoyable, loaded with inventive sight gags. The sequence with Martin trying to help Lewis stuff his parachute properly is a gem. (1952, black and white, not rated.)

MY FRIEND IRMA. Marie Wilson's bubbleheaded title character, from her popular radio show, provided Martin and Lewis with their first film appearance, and they handily steal the show. (1949, black and white, not rated.)

SCARED STIFF. Enjoyable horror-comedy, actually a remake of Bob Hope's *Ghost Breakers,* with Martin and Lewis encountering zombies at a spooky Cuban mansion. Lewis and Carmen Miranda provide most of the laughs here. (1953, black and white, not rated.)

DRAMAS

DOMESTIC
...

AVALON. Superb storytelling from writer-director Barry Levinson, who takes a fictional look at his own immigrant roots through the story of an old man remembering his life. Subtext includes a strong statement about how television affects our lives. Aidan Quinn, Elizabeth Perkins, Armin Mueller-Stahl, Joan Plowright. (1990, color, PG, profanity.)

BLOSSOMS IN THE DUST. Greer Garson loses her husband and child, prompting her to form an orphanage in Texas. Fairly typical golden-era weeper, given a boost by Garson and Technicolor cinematography. Walter Pidgeon. (1941, color, not rated.)

THE ENCHANTED COTTAGE. Lovely romantic fantasy about an unattractive woman (Dorothy McGuire) and a disfigured man (Robert Young) who meet, see each other's inner beauty, and fall in love. (1945, black and white, not rated.)

PENNY SERENADE. Romance, tragedy, and survival are among the things Irene Dunne remembers about her marriage to Cary Grant as she contemplates divorce in this first-rate soap opera. (1941, black and white, not rated.)

THE QUIET MAN. John Wayne and Maureen O'Hara make a feisty pair in this comedy-romance, an atypical John Ford film. Wayne is an American ex-boxer who returns to the land of his fathers and sets his sights on quick-tempered O'Hara. Gorgeously photographed, great support from Barry Fitzgerald, Victor McLaglen, Ward Bond. (1952, color, not rated.)

SOUNDER. Superbly performed, sensitively realized look at black sharecroppers during the Depression, focusing on the struggles of a family whose father is sent to jail. Cicely Tyson, Paul Winfield, Kevin Hooks. (1972, color, G; the sequel, *Sounder, Part 2* is not on video.)

TENDER MERCIES. Superb, Oscar-winning performance by Robert Duvall highlights this excellent story of a former alcoholic country singer who is redeemed by love when he meets a young widow (Tess Harper) and her son. Ellen Barkin, Wilford Brimley. (1983, color, PG, profanity.)

HALLMARK HALL OF FAME
...

CAROLINE? Thriller, with Stephanie Zimbalist in the title role. A daughter presumed dead for fifteen years returns to reclaim an inheritance, but is she really who she says she is? Pamela Reed, Patricia Neal, Dorothy McGuire. (1990, color, PG, violence.)

DECORATION DAY. James Garner gives a fine performance in this TV-movie about a retired judge who tries to find out why an old friend has refused the Medal of Honor. Bill Cobbs, Larry Fishburne, Judith Ivey, Ruby Dee. (1990, color, PG, violence.)

FOXFIRE. This production stars Jessica Tandy (who won an Emmy and, previously, a Tony for playing the same role on Broadway) as an aging woman who has lived her life in the Blue Ridge Mountains and won't move, despite the urgings of her son (John Denver). Hume Cronyn costars as the late husband with whom she still converses. (1987, color, not rated.)

70

O PIONEERS! In this heartfelt film, Jessica Lange stars as a head-strong Nebraska homesteader who lets love pass her by so she can keep the family farm going. (1992, color, PG, adult themes.)

SARAH, PLAIN AND TALL. Very good story of a mail-order bride (Glenn Close) who touches the life of the Kansas widower (Christopher Walken) who sends for her. (1990, color, G.)

THE SECRET GARDEN. Very popular TV version of the classic story. An orphan finds a garden her uncle has walled up on his estate and sets about putting it back in order. (1987, color, not rated.)

JUVENILE DELINQUENCY
...

ANGELS WITH DIRTY FACES. The classic story of boyhood friends who grow up to go different ways, one becoming a priest (Pat O'Brien) working with delinquent youth and the other a gangster (James Cagney), whom the boys admire. Old message film bolstered by terrific cast. Humphrey Bogart, Ann Sheridan, Leo Gorcey, Huntz Hall. (1938, black and white, not rated.)

THE BLACKBOARD JUNGLE. In this tough drama, Glenn Ford is a new, idealistic teacher in a rough New York City school, with young Sidney Poitier, Vic Morrow, future director Paul Mazursky, and Jamie Farr among his students. Anne Francis. (1955, black and white, not rated.)

BOYS' TOWN/MEN OF BOYS' TOWN. Sentimental but enjoyable films about Father Flanagan (Spencer Tracy, who won an Oscar) and his school for delinquent boys, with Mickey Rooney as the chief delinquent. (1938/1941, black and white, not rated.)

MY BODYGUARD. Funny, witty look at a picked-on young boy (Chris Makepeace) who hires a big kid in school (Adam Baldwin) to protect him from bullies. Martin Mull, Ruth Gordon, Matt Dillon. (1980, color, PG, violence, profanity).

REBEL WITHOUT A CAUSE. Excellent story of alienated youth with James Dean as the archetypical title character, trying to find some meaning in his life. Dean, Sal Mineo, and Natalie Wood are standouts, though everyone is good here. Dennis Hopper, Nick Adams. (1955, color, not rated.)

STAND AND DELIVER. A top-notch lead performance by Edward James Olmos gives force to this true story of a teacher who tries to inspire his poverty-ridden students to pass an advanced calculus test. Lou Diamond Phillips, Andy Garcia. (1987, color, PG, violence, profanity.)

TO SIR, WITH LOVE. Sidney Poitier is great as the new teacher in school who tries to reach tough teens in London's East End. Judy Geeson, Suzy Kendall, Lulu. (1967, color, not rated.)

BIOGRAPHIES
■■■

CROSS CREEK. Mary Steenburgen plays author Marjorie Kinnan Rawlings (*The Yearling*), who moved to the Florida swamplands to grow oranges and look for writing inspiration among the simple people there. Inspiring family film. (1983, color, PG, violence, profanity.)

THE EDDY DUCHIN STORY. Tyrone Power takes the title role in this glossy, sentimental biography of the pianist/bandleader. Kim Novak, James Whitmore. (1956, color, not rated.)

84 CHARING CROSS ROAD. Warm and witty true story of a New York woman's correspondence and growing friendship over many years with a British bookseller who provides her with rare books. Anne Bancroft and Anthony Hopkins are superb in the leads. (1987, color, PG, profanity.)

THE ELEPHANT MAN. Stirring true story of hideously deformed John Merrick (John Hurt), who is taken in by a doctor (Anthony Hopkins) for hospital study. May be frightening for very young children. (1980, black and white, PG, violence.)

THE FIVE PENNIES. Danny Kaye plays it straight in this sentimental musical biography of jazz trumpeter Red Nichols. Kaye's duets with Louis Armstrong are especially winning. Barbara Bel Geddes, Tuesday Weld. (1959, color, not rated.)

GANDHI. Superb epic tale of the peacemaker whose message helped gain India's independence and who set an example to the world. Oscar-winner Ben Kingsley delivers a one-of-a-kind performance here. Candice Bergen, Edward Fox, John Gielgud,

Trevor Howard, John Mills, Martin Sheen. Two tapes. (1982, color, not rated.)

THE GREAT IMPOSTER. Hollywoodized but fun look at Ferdinand Demara, who successfully masqueraded as a doctor, Harvard research fellow, prison warden, and so on. Tony Curtis is energetic in the role. Edmond O'Brien, Karl Malden. (1961, black and white, not rated.)

HOUDINI. The re-creations of the great magician's escapes are the most interesting aspect of this colorful but superficial biography. Tony Curtis is good in the title role; Janet Leigh costars. (1953, color, not rated.)

THE LONG GRAY LINE. John Ford's sentimental look at the life of Marty Maher, an Irish immigrant who found a long career at West Point as an athletic trainer. Tyrone Power and Maureen O'Hara are good in the leads. (1955, color, not rated.)

MAN OF A THOUSAND FACES. James Cagney is very good as silent star Lon Chaney in this melodrama that includes re-creations of many famous movie sequences, from *The Phantom of the Opera* to *The Hunchback of Notre Dame.* Dorothy Malone, Jane Greer. (1957, black and white, not rated.)

THE MIRACLE WORKER. Both the '60s original and the TV remake of Helen Keller's biography are worth a look, both based on the Broadway play about Anne Sullivan taming the blind, deaf child and becoming her teacher and companion. The first film stars Anne Bancroft as Sullivan and young Patty Duke as Keller (both won Oscars); the second casts Duke as Sullivan and Melissa Gilbert as Keller. (1962, black and white, not rated/1979, color, not rated.)

THE SPIRIT OF ST. LOUIS. James Stewart is great as Charles Lindbergh in this account of his famed flight across the Atlantic. (1957, color, not rated.)

SUNRISE AT CAMPOBELLO. Ralph Bellamy reprises his Tony-winning Broadway triumph as President Franklin Roosevelt, and Greer Garson is his wife Eleanor in this dramatic look at his politics and bout with polio. Hume Cronyn. (1960, color, not rated.)

CHARLES DICKENS

•••

DAVID COPPERFIELD. Lavish production values and great cast make this a superb effort at capturing Dickens on film, with great characterizations in the story of the title character's life from childhood on. Freddie Bartholomew, W. C. Fields, Lionel Barrymore, Roland Young, Basil Rathbone, Maureen O'Sullivan. (1935, black and white, not rated.)

GREAT EXPECTATIONS. Superb David Lean adaptation of the Dickens novel, with John Mills as the adult Pip, who goes from rags to unexpected riches. Valerie Hobson, Alec Guinness, Jean Simmons. (1946, black and white, not rated.)

OLIVER TWIST. David Lean's classic film of the famous novel, with Alec Guinness as Fagin and young Anthony Newley as the Artful Dodger in the story of an innocent orphan caught up with criminal elements. Robert Newton. (1948, black and white, not rated; also recommendable are the 1982 made-for-TV version with George C. Scott and a 1922 silent version with Jackie Coogan and Lon Chaney.)

VICTOR HUGO

•••

THE HUNCHBACK OF NOTRE DAME. Three versions are available on video, and all are worth a look. The first is a silent classic with Lon Chaney; the second stars Charles Laughton and Maureen O'Hara and is very well made; the third, a made-for-TV version, is also excellent, with Anthony Hopkins quite good in the lead. (1923/1939, black and white, not rated; 1982, color, not rated.)

LES MISERABLES. Two excellent versions are available: the older classic with Fredric March as the petty thief hounded by a policeman (Charles Laughton), and the second a made-for-TV film with Richard Jordan and Anthony Perkins in those respective roles. Both are very well acted. (1935, black and white, not rated; 1978, color, not rated.)

OTHER LITERARY ADAPTATIONS

•••

ANNE OF GREEN GABLES/ANNE OF AVONLEA. Two superb Canadian miniseries, based on the books by Lucy Maud Montgomery, starring Megan Follows. (1985/1987, color, not rated.)

THE CAINE MUTINY. Humphrey Bogart steals the show as paranoid, autocratic Captain Queeg, whose petulant behavior prompts his crew to mutiny, with subsequent court-martial casting doubts on the action. Great cast includes Jose Ferrer, Van Johnson, Fred MacMurray, E. G. Marshall, Lee Marvin. (1954, color, not rated.)

CAPTAINS COURAGEOUS. Spencer Tracy (who won an Oscar) is a Portuguese fisherman who rescues a spoiled, rich kid (Freddie Bartholomew) and teaches him about life. Excellent version of Kipling's story, with Melvyn Douglas, Lionel Barrymore, Mickey Rooney, and John Carradine in support. (1937, black and white, not rated.)

FRIENDLY PERSUASION. Eloquent look at gentle Quaker life in Indiana prior to the Civil War and the way that the outbreak of violence around them disrupts their lives. Excellent performances from Gary Cooper, Dorothy McGuire, Anthony Perkins, Majorie Main. (1956, color, not rated.)

GONE WITH THE WIND. Epic look at the changing Old South during the Civil War, focusing on selfish Southern belle Scarlett O'Hara (played perfectly by Vivien Leigh, who won an Oscar) and gadabout Rhett Butler (Clark Gable). Leslie Howard, Olivia de Havilland. (1939, color, not rated.)

GOODBYE, MR. CHIPS. Classic, Oscar-winning story of a shy schoolmaster (Robert Donat) devoted to the students at his boys school, finding love with Greer Garson. Paul Henreid, John Mills. (1939, black and white, not rated; the 1969 color musical remake, with Peter O'Toole and Petula Clark, is also available, though it's not nearly as good.)

GUNGA DIN. Rousing adventure and comedy with Cary Grant, Victor McLaglen, and Douglas Fairbanks as soldiers in nineteenth-century India doing battle with the thuggee cult. Great fun; Sam Jaffe has the title role. (1939, black and white, not rated.)

Vivien Leigh and Clark Gable in *Gone with the Wind*. ©1939 Turner Entertainment
Company. All rights reserved. Used by permission.

JANE EYRE. Joan Fontaine is the orphan who eventually becomes
governess to Orson Welles's brooding household in this rich
adaptation of the Charlotte Brontë novel. Margaret O'Brien, Elizabeth Taylor. (1944, black and white, not rated.)

KING'S ROW. Sweeping soap-opera tale of life in middle America,
focusing on a young psychiatrist (Robert Cummings) in the midst
of nasty goings-on in his home town. Ronald Reagan (in what
is considered his finest hour) costars, along with Ann Sheridan,
Betty Field, Charles Coburn, Claude Rains, Judith Anderson.
(1942, black and white, not rated.)

THE MAGNIFICENT AMBERSONS. Orson Welles's classic view of the
downfall of a wealthy American family unwilling to change with
the times is a fabulous film in all respects. Joseph Cotten, Tim
Holt, Dolores Costello, Anne Baxter. (1942, black and white, not
rated.)

MOBY DICK. Gregory Peck is Captain Ahab in lifelong pursuit of
the great white whale. Interesting adaptation of Melville's classic

Hayley Mills, left, and Jane Wyman, right, in *Pollyanna*. ©Buena Vista Pictures Distribution. Used by permission.

novel, directed by John Huston. Richard Basehart, Orson Welles. (1956, color, not rated.)

POLLYANNA. Hayley Mills won an Oscar for her portrayal of the ever-sunny young lady who moves in with her sour aunt (Jane Wyman) and has an exuberant effect on the locals in a small New England town. (1960, color, not rated.)

PRIDE AND PREJUDICE. Five sisters in early nineteenth-century England go hunting for husbands, with independent Greer Garson keen on Laurence Olivier. Great cast in literate adaptation of the Jane Austen novel. Edna May Oliver, Edmund Gwenn, Maureen O'Sullivan. (1940, black and white, not rated.)

RANDOM HARVEST. Great amnesia soap opera with Ronald Colman losing his memory and wife Greer Garson trying to help him get it back. Very well acted and directed. (1942, black and white, not rated.)

REBECCA. Classic story of a young woman (Joan Fontaine) who marries a nobleman (Laurence Olivier) only to find she must live in the shadow of his first wife. Great performances under the direction of Alfred Hitchcock. Judith Anderson, George Sanders. (1940, black and white, not rated.)

THE TREASURE OF THE SIERRA MADRE. Fabulous Oscar-winning masterpiece holds up as the ultimate antigreed movie, with Humphrey Bogart, Walter Huston, and Tim Holt as prospectors looking for gold in Mexico. Superbly directed by John Huston, who has a cameo as an American tourist. (1948, black and white, not rated.)

A TREE GROWS IN BROOKLYN. This evocative look at a blue-collar family living in a Brooklyn tenement at the turn of the century has lost none of its power or charm, with standout performances by Dorothy McGuire as the strong-willed mother, James Dunn as the alcoholic father, and Peggy Ann Garner as the young girl hoping for a better life. (1945, black and white, not rated.)

WUTHERING HEIGHTS. The classic version with Laurence Olivier as Heathcliff and Merle Oberon as Cathy is unbeatable, with splendid performances and sweeping direction in this story of doomed love. The remake with Timothy Dalton isn't bad, however. (1939, black and white, not rated/1970, color, G.)

OTHERS
■■■

CONRACK. Uplifting true story of a white teacher (Jon Voight) trying to earn respect of parents and students when he's assigned to an all-black South Carolina school. Paul Winfield, Hume Cronyn, Madge Sinclair. (1974, color, PG, violence, profanity.)

CRY FREEDOM. Richard Attenborough's epic look at the friendship of South African activist Steve Biko (Denzel Washington) and white reporter Donald Woods (Kevin Kline) is harrowing and timely. Too stark for young children, but a good lesson on apartheid for teens. (1987, color, PG, violence, profanity.)

DRIVING MISS DAISY. Warm, witty Oscar-winning story of relationship between headstrong older white woman (Jessica Tandy) and her black chauffeur (Morgan Freeman) in the South over a twenty-five-year period. Dan Aykroyd, Patti LuPone, Esther Rolle. (1989, color, PG, one profanity.)

EYE ON THE SPARROW. A blind couple (Mare Winningham, Keith Carradine) try to adopt a child in this true story, bolstered by the stars' riveting performances. Made for TV. (1987, color, PG, adult themes.)

GOING MY WAY/THE BELLS OF ST. MARY'S. Bing Crosby stars in these two stories of Father O'Malley, winning over his cranky superior (Barry Fitzgerald) in the first and a stubborn mother superior (Ingrid Bergman) in the second. Both are good, but the first is superb (Crosby and Fitzgerald both won Oscars). (1944/ 1944, black and white, not rated.)

THE LONG WALK HOME. Whoopi Goldberg delivers a superb performance in this examination of the mid-'50s bus boycott by the black community of Montgomery, Alabama, and its effect on the families of a maid (Goldberg) and her uppercrust employer (Sissy Spacek). (1990, color, PG, violence.)

SEPARATE BUT EQUAL. Excellent made-for-TV drama, the true story of racial tensions in the South erupting over school busing in the mid-'50s, with lawyer Thurgood Marshall (Sidney Poitier) arguing the case in the Supreme Court. Burt Lancaster, Richard Kiley. (1991, color, PG, violence.)

MUSICALS
■■■■■■■■■■■■■■■■■■■■■■■■■■■■■■■■■■■ ■ ■

ASTAIRE AND ROGERS
■■■

Before going on to further heights separately, Fred Astaire and Ginger Rogers starred together in nine musicals from 1933 to 1938, then teamed up once more ten years later. Their films were mostly bright comedies, highlighted by exquisite dance sequences. All ten films are on video:

THE BARKLEYS OF BROADWAY. Bright tale of squabbling show-biz couple, with some very good songs. The only Astaire-Rogers film in color. Oscar Levant, Billie Burke. (1949, color, not rated.)

CAREFREE. Easily their goofiest outing, with Astaire a psychiatrist and Rogers his eccentric patient. Irving Berlin songs. Ralph Bellamy, Jack Carson. (1938, black and white, not rated.)

FLYING DOWN TO RIO. Their first teaming—and they aren't the stars of the film. But when Astaire and Rogers dance together, you can still feel the magic of their on-screen chemistry. Famous moment has chorus girls dancing on the wings of a plane. (1933, black and white, not rated.)

FOLLOW THE FLEET. One of their best films. Astaire and Randolph Scott are sailors romancing a pair of sisters (Rogers, Harriet Hilliard). Great Irving Berlin score. Look for Betty Grable and Lucille Ball in support; Hilliard became the latter half of "Ozzie and Harriet." (1936, black and white, not rated.)

THE GAY DIVORCEE. Zany comedy of mistaken identity involving a would-be divorcee (Rogers) pursued by a lovesick author (Astaire). Edward Everett Horton, Betty Grable. (1934, black and white, not rated.)

ROBERTA. So-so musical of an American troupe of entertainers stuck running a Parisian dress shop, but the film really takes off whenever supporting players Astaire and Rogers show up. Great songs. One sequence is in color; look fast for Lucille Ball. Irene Dunne, Randolph Scott. (1935, black and white, not rated.)

SHALL WE DANCE. Gershwin songs liven this routine comedy about a pair of dancing partners who pretend to be married. Edward Everett Horton. (1937, black and white, not rated.)

THE STORY OF VERNON AND IRENE CASTLE. True story of a famous dance duo in the early part of the century who gain fame in Paris and become international celebrities. Lots of nostalgic songs. Walter Brennan. (1939, black and white, not rated.)

SWING TIME. Astaire and Rogers at the top of their form, with great songs backing them up in the story of a dance team falling in love—but he's engaged to the girl back home. (1936, black and white, not rated.)

TOP HAT. Considered by critics to be Astaire and Rogers's best film. He chases her from London to Paris, while she thinks he's married to her best friend. Great Irving Berlin score. Edward

Everett Horton; Lucille Ball has a bit. (1935, black and white, not rated.)

RODGERS AND HAMMERSTEIN
...

Richard Rodgers and Oscar Hammerstein wrote some of the best-loved musical productions of all time, and they remain popular items on video. These eight are chock-full of memorable songs:

CAROUSEL. Perhaps the best of the film adaptations, with gorgeous Maine locations and those superlative songs. Gordon MacRae and Shirley Jones costar in their second Rodgers and Hammerstein outing, the story of a tough carousel barker who returns from the dead to redeem himself with the family he wronged on Earth. (1956, color, not rated.)

CINDERELLA. Lesley Ann Warren stars in this made-for-TV version of the fairy tale, with Celeste Holm, Jo Van Fleet, Ginger Rogers, and Walter Pidgeon. (1964, color, not rated.)

FLOWER DRUM SONG. Lesser Rodgers and Hammerstein material, but still an enjoyable look at Asian culture in a changing world. Set in San Francisco's Chinatown. Nancy Kwan, James Shigeta, Miyoshi Umeki. (1961, color, not rated.)

THE KING AND I. Yul Brynner will forever be identified with his role as the King of Siam in this great musical, with Deborah Kerr as the Englishwoman who comes to teach his many children. (Kerr's singing voice is dubbed by Marni Nixon.) Rita Moreno. (1956, color, not rated.)

OKLAHOMA! Terrific adaptation of the Western musical, with Shirley Jones and Gordon MacRae perfect in the leads and great support from Rod Steiger, Gene Nelson, Gloria Graham, Charlotte Greenwood, Eddie Albert, James Whitmore, and Jay C. Flippen. (1955, color, not rated.)

SOUTH PACIFIC. Mitzi Gaynor gives a sprightly performance as the Navy nurse romanced by an older man (Rossano Brazzi, with his singing voice dubbed by Giorgio Tozzi) in this popular May-December romance. The songs are great, but as a film it isn't quite up to other Rodgers-Hammerstein adaptations. Ray Walston, France Nuyen, Juanita Hall. (1958, color, not rated.)

STATE FAIR. Good songs (the only Rodgers and Hammerstein score written specifically for the screen) brighten this bit of Americana set at the Iowa State Fair. The earlier version, with Jeanne Crain, Dana Andrews, Dick Haymes, and Vivian Blaine is the one to see. The remake, with Pat Boone, Bobby Darin, Pamela Tiffin, Ann-Margret, and Alice Faye is weak. (1945/1962, color, not rated.)

THE SOUND OF MUSIC. The Oscar-winning story of the Von Trapp Family Singers, with Julie Andrews, Christopher Plummer, and brood, is one of the most popular films of all time. Two tapes. (1965, color, not rated.)

BROADWAY'S BEST
...

ANNIE. The stage hit based on the "Little Orphan Annie" comic strip is too big and tries too hard, but it is still enjoyable, with Albert Finney as Daddy Warbucks, Carol Burnett as Mrs. Hannigan, and Aileen Quinn as Annie. Directed by John Huston. (1982, color, PG, profanity.)

THE BAND WAGON. A very funny backstage musical with Fred Astaire as a movie star tackling Broadway. Great support from Cyd Charisse, Oscar Levant, Nanette Fabray, Jack Buchanan. (1953, color, not rated.)

THE BOY FRIEND. Charming homage to Hollywood musicals of old, particularly Busby Berkeley, with a winning performance by Twiggy. (1971, color, G.)

BRIGADOON. New Yorkers Gene Kelly and Van Johnson find themselves in a Scottish village that appears only once a century in this delightful fantasy with memorable Lerner and Loewe songs. (1954, color, not rated.)

BYE BYE BIRDIE. Parody of Elvis being drafted and the mayhem caused by his fans is a bit dated now, and the movie unwisely tried to turn it into a young Ann-Margret vehicle, but the best songs survive, and Dick Van Dyke and Paul Lynde, reprising their stage roles, are great. Janet Leigh, Maureen Stapleton, Bobby Rydell, Ed Sullivan. (1963, color, not rated.)

CABIN IN THE SKY. Broadway show is dated (and, to some degree, racist) but does afford an opportunity to see some of the great black artists of the '40s, including Lena Horne, Ethel Waters, Louis Armstrong, Rex Ingram, and Duke Ellington. Story has heavenly forces vying for the soul of Eddie "Rochester" Anderson. (1943, black and white, not rated.)

FIDDLER ON THE ROOF. Poor Jewish farmers struggle to preserve their heritage in a small village in the Ukraine at the turn of the century. Wonderful, location-shot musical, with Topol as Tevye. Two tapes. (1971, color, G.)

FINIAN'S RAINBOW. Francis Ford Coppola directed this story of an Irishman (Fred Astaire), his daughter (Petula Clark), and a leprechaun (Tommy Steele), who come to America. Al Freeman, Jr., is excellent in the racial injustice subplot. (1968, color, G.)

FUNNY GIRL. Barbra Streisand won an Oscar and became a star with her first movie role, re-creating her stage success as Fanny Brice, in this terrific musical-comedy, with Omar Sharif as the gangster she marries. (1968, color, G.)

GUYS AND DOLLS. Stylized big-screen adaptation of the gangsters and gambling musical. Frank Sinatra is Nathan Detroit, and Marlon Brando is Sky Masterson, with Stubby Kaye stealing the show. Terrific Frank Loesser songs. Jean Simmons, Vivian Blaine. (1955, color, not rated.)

HOW TO SUCCEED IN BUSINESS WITHOUT REALLY TRYING. Bright and witty musical comedy, with fine songs and production numbers in story of a window-washer Robert Morse who reads the title book to get ahead in business. Michele Lee, Rudy Vallee. (1967, color, not rated.)

LI'L ABNER. On film, the stage musical of Al Capp's comic strip is loud and corny but undeniably energetic. Stubby Kaye steals the show as Marryin' Sam. Peter Palmer, Leslie Parrish, Julie Newmar, Stella Stevens; Jerry Lewis has a cameo bit. (1959, color, not rated.)

THE MUSIC MAN. Witty, tuneful Meredith Willson tale of Professor Harold Hill, a con man selling musical instruments for a children's band to skeptical parents in a small, Iowa town. A knockout performance by Robert Preston, reprising his stage triumph, but everyone is good here. Shirley Jones, Buddy Hackett, Ronny Howard. (1962, color, not rated.)

MY FAIR LADY. Rex Harrison and Audrey Hepburn (with her singing dubbed by Marni Nixon) star in this lavish adaptation of the Lerner and Loewe stage hit. Winner of eight Oscars. Two tapes. (1964, color, G.)

OLIVER! Excellent adaptation of the musical stage version of Dickens's *Oliver Twist*, with great songs, sets, and performances, especially Ron Moody as Fagin. Oliver Reed, Mark Lester, Jack Wild. (1968, color, not rated.)

THE PAJAMA GAME. Doris Day shines in this fast-paced film version of the stage play. Workers in a pajama factory are about to strike when their spokesperson falls for the boss (John Raitt). Great songs and dance numbers (with choreography by Bob Fosse). (1957, color, not rated.)

1776. Most of the stage cast reprises its roles for this adaptation of the song-filled retelling of the efforts of the Continental Congress to ratify the Declaration of Independence. William Daniels, Howard da Silva, Ken Howard, Blythe Danner. (1972, color, G.)

SHOW BOAT. Two versions of this classic Kern and Hammerstein musical are on video, the first being the best (with Irene Dunne, Allan Jones, Helen Morgan, and Paul Robeson) but the second being the most popular (with Kathryn Grayson, Howard Keel, Ava Gardner, and William Warfield). (1936/1951, black and white/color, not rated.)

SILK STOCKINGS. Good remake of comedy *Ninotchka*, with Cyd Charisse as the Russian agent who unexpectedly falls in love with happy-go-lucky Fred Astaire in Paris, adding music to the mix. (1957, color, not rated.)

THE UNSINKABLE MOLLY BROWN. One of Debbie Reynolds's best-loved films, a big, rowdy adaptation of Meredith Willson's stage hit, based on the true story of a backwoods gal who tried to become part of Denver's society crowd. Harve Presnell. (1964, color, not rated.)

WEST SIDE STORY. One of the great Broadway adaptations, with memorable score by Leonard Bernstein and Stephen Sondheim, starring Natalie Wood (Marni Nixon dubbed her singing voice), Richard Beymer, George Chakiris, Rita Moreno, Russ Tamblyn in update of *Romeo and Juliet* as a gang melodrama. Terrific use of New York locations; winner of ten Oscars. (1961, color, not rated.)

MADE FOR THE SILVER SCREEN
...

AN AMERICAN IN PARIS. Gene Kelly at the peak of his form in a film built around Gershwin music. Features Kelly's famous ballet finale. Leslie Caron, Oscar Levant. (1951, color, not rated.)

ANCHORS AWEIGH. Good comic yarn of two sailors (Gene Kelly, Frank Sinatra) on leave, with terrific musical numbers, highlighted by Kelly's dance with Jerry the cartoon mouse. Kathryn Grayson. (1945, color, not rated.)

A DATE WITH JUDY. Old-fashioned comedy with sprightly musical numbers and Elizabeth Taylor as a teenager. Wallace Beery, Carmen Miranda, Jane Powell. (1948, color, not rated.)

EASTER PARADE. The Irving Berlin songs help this story of song-and-dance man Fred Astaire fighting with one partner (Ann Miller) while landing another (Judy Garland). Peter Lawford. (1948, color, not rated.)

GIGI. Lovely adaptation of the French story of a young tomboy who has love on her mind. A very nice Lerner and Loewe score; winner of nine Oscars. Leslie Caron, Maurice Chevalier, Louis Jourdan, Hermione Gingold. (1958, color, not rated.)

THE GREAT CARUSO. Fans of the opera legend will enjoy this Hollywood biography with Mario Lanza and Ann Blyth. (1951, color, not rated.)

THE HARVEY GIRLS. Western musical comedy with Judy Garland

Dick Van Dyke, left, and Julie Andrews, right, in an animated scene from *Mary Poppins.* ©Buena Vista Pictures Distribution. Used by permission.

as a mail-order bride who works as a waitress at Fred Harvey's restaurants, meeting up with Ray Bolger, Angela Lansbury, Marjorie Main, and others. (1946, color, not rated.)

HIGH SOCIETY. Nice musical remake (with sparkling Cole Porter songs) of *The Philadelphia Story,* with Grace Kelly (in her final role), Bing Crosby, and Frank Sinatra in the leads. Celeste Holm, Louis Armstrong. (1956, color, not rated.)

LILI. Charming musical of French orphan Leslie Caron, who joins a traveling carnival and falls for a magician while enchanted by the puppets of an embittered puppeteer (Mel Ferrer). Zsa Zsa Gabor. (1953, color, not rated.)

MARY POPPINS. The knockout, Oscar-winning Disney tale of a magical nanny who touches the lives of a London family, with the assistance of a chimney sweep. Brilliant animated sequences. Julie Andrews (who won an Oscar as best actress) and Dick Van Dyke. (1964, color, not rated.)

MEET ME IN ST. LOUIS. The 1903 World's Fair is the setting for this fine collection of memorable songs and set pieces, with Judy Garland, Mary Astor, Marjorie Main, and little Margaret O'Brien, who steals the show. (1944, color, not rated.)

ON THE TOWN. Excellent comedy about three sailors (Gene Kelly, Frank Sinatra, Jules Munshin), who are on leave in New York, in search of "Miss Turnstile." Vera-Ellen, Betty Garrett, Ann Miller. (1949, color, not rated.)

THE PIRATE. Splashy musical with Judy Garland mistaking a circus clown (Gene Kelly) for a notorious pirate. Good Cole Porter songs and choreography. (1948, color, not rated.)

POPEYE. Funny, if cluttered, comic-strip musical from Robert Altman, with Robin Williams and especially Shelley Duvall perfect as Popeye and Olive Oyl. (1980, color, G.)

ROBIN AND THE SEVEN HOODS. Amusing update of "Robin Hood," with Frank Sinatra and his "Rat Pack" as Chicago gangsters during the '20s. Dean Martin, Sammy Davis, Jr., Bing Crosby, Peter Falk, Edward G. Robinson; features the song "My Kind of Town." (1964, color, not rated.)

ROYAL WEDDING. Fred Astaire and Jane Powell are a brother-sister act in London for Queen Elizabeth II's wedding, with some of Astaire's best dance routines. Peter Lawford, Keenan Wynn. (1951, color, not rated.)

SEVEN BRIDES FOR SEVEN BROTHERS. Raucous classic is a wonderful original, with fur-trapper Howard Keel taking Jane Powell as his wife, causing no end of envy from his roughneck brothers. Great dance sequences highlight this gem. (1954, color, not rated.)

THE SEVEN LITTLE FOYS. Hollywood biography of stage entertainer Eddie Foy (Bob Hope) and his show-biz brood; James Cagney has a scene as George M. Cohan, his *Yankee Doodle Dandy* character. (1954, color, not rated.)

SINGIN' IN THE RAIN. Considered by most critics to be the best musical ever made, with a hilarious plot about silent movies being usurped by talkies. Gene Kelly, Debbie Reynolds, and Donald O'Connor are in great form; O'Connor all but steals the show with the "Make 'Em Laugh" number. (1952, color, not rated.)

STARS AND STRIPES FOREVER. Clifton Webb stars as John Philip

Sousa in this popular biography of the marching tune composer. (1952, color, not rated.)

STORMY WEATHER. Try to forget the silly backstage yarn with its unsuccessful romantic pairing of Lena Horne and Bill "Bojangles" Robinson and just enjoy the musical numbers, including Horne singing the title tune and Fats Waller's great "Ain't Misbehavin'." Cab Calloway, Fats Waller, Dooley Wilson, the Nicholas Brothers. (1943, black and white, not rated.)

THAT'S ENTERTAINMENT!/THAT'S ENTERTAINMENT, PART 2. These two films, reviewing highlights from MGM's musicals (and, in the second, comedies and dramas), are utterly entrancing and provide a terrific way to introduce youngsters to the glories of musical comedy. (1974/1976, color, G.)

THERE'S NO BUSINESS LIKE SHOW BUSINESS. Irving Berlin songs and elaborate production numbers enliven this tale of a showbiz family on the road, with Ethel Merman, Dan Dailey, Donald O'Connor, Marilyn Monroe, Mitzi Gaynor. (1954, color, not rated.)

THEY SHALL HAVE MUSIC. Fascinating effort to spread the gospel of classical music and showcase Jascha Heifetz; his violin playing provides the film's highlights in this tale of a failing music school run by Walter Brennan. Joel McCrea, Marjorie Main. (1939, black and white, not rated.)

THOROUGHLY MODERN MILLIE. Julie Andrews and Mary Tyler Moore team for this flapper-era comedy of two innocent young women on the loose in the big city. Good production numbers, though the film is too long. (1967, color, not rated.)

THREE LITTLE WORDS. Fred Astaire and Red Skelton are a fine team in this story of songwriters Kalmar and Ruby, with great songs and a wonderful supporting cast of Vera-Ellen, Arlene Dahl, Keenan Wynn, Gloria DeHaven, and Debbie Reynolds. (1950, color, not rated.)

TWO WEEKS WITH LOVE. Debbie Reynolds and Carleton Carpenter's duet of "Abba Dabba Honeymoon" is the highlight of this musical about a family vacation in the Catskills. Jane Powell, Ricardo Montalban. (1950, color, not rated.)

Dorothy (Judy Garland), the Tin Woodsman (Jack Haley), the Cowardly Lion (Bert Lahr), and the Scarecrow (Ray Bolger) in *The Wizard of Oz*. ©1939 Turner Entertainment Company. All rights reserved. Used by permission.

THE WIZARD OF OZ. This timeless fantasy just gets better all the time. If you haven't watched Dorothy's trip down the yellow brick road lately, take another look. Judy Garland, Ray Bolger, Jack Haley, Bert Lahr, Margaret Hamilton. (1939, color/black and white, not rated.)

YANKEE DOODLE DANDY. James Cagney won his Oscar for this terrific biography of George M. Cohan, who was born on the Fourth of July and became a zealous patriot on the musical stage. (1942, black and white, not rated.)

ACTION/ADVENTURE

THE ADVENTURES OF ROBIN HOOD. Terrific derring-do, with Errol Flynn in top form as the bandit who robs from the rich and gives

89

to the poor. Olivia de Havilland, Basil Rathbone, Claude Rains. (1938, color, not rated.)

THE CHARGE OF THE LIGHT BRIGADE. Lavish, romantic, action-filled look at the British cavalry in India, with Errol Flynn deliberately starting a war to even an old score. Olivia de Havilland, Nigel Bruce, David Niven. (1936, black and white, not rated.)

THE COUNT OF MONTE CRISTO. Rousing action, based on the classic yarn about an innocent man who is imprisoned but eventually escapes and seeks revenge on those who framed him. Robert Donat is terrific in the lead. (1934, black and white, not rated.)

THE FLAME AND THE ARROW. Burt Lancaster is at his most acrobatic as a rebel trying to overthrow a tyrant in medieval Italy. Virginia Mayo. (1950, color, not rated.)

FLIGHT OF THE PHOENIX. Gripping drama of survivors of a plane crash in the Arabian desert, with James Stewart and Richard Attenborough trying to hold things together. Peter Finch, Hardy Kruger, Ernest Borgnine, Dan Duryea, George Kennedy. (1966, color, not rated.)

HATARI! John Wayne heads the cast in this Africa adventure comedy, rounding up wild animals with help from Elsa Martinelli and Red Buttons. (1962, color, not rated.)

THE PRINCE AND THE PAUPER. Errol Flynn and Claude Rains headline this adaptation of Mark Twain's yarn about a prince and a poor boy (Billy and Bobby Mauch) who trade places, with loads of action. (1937, black and white, not rated.)

SCARAMOUCHE. Stewart Granger is the swordfighting hero seeking revenge for the death of his friend while masquerading as an actor during the French Revolution. The six-and-a-half minute sword duel climax is the longest in film history. (1952, color, not rated.)

WARGAMES. A young computer wizard accidentally taps into America's nuclear-defense system, thinks he's playing a high-tech video game, and nearly causes World War III. Wild comedy thriller with appealing cast. Matthew Broderick, Dabney Coleman, Ally Sheedy. (1983, color, PG, profanity, violence.)

THE HIGH SEAS

■■■

CAPTAIN BLOOD. Errol Flynn's first swashbuckler, about a doctor forced to become a pirate, is one of the best of the breed. Olivia de Havilland, Basil Rathbone, Lionel Atwill. (1935, black and white, not rated.)

THE CRIMSON PIRATE. Funny and exciting swashbuckler with athletic Burt Lancaster as an eighteenth-century pirate leading oppressed people on an island to freedom. (1952, color, not rated.)

THE HUNT FOR RED OCTOBER. Tense thriller set largely underwater as Russian captain Sean Connery pilots his nuclear sub toward the United States. Alec Baldwin is the CIA analyst who thinks he knows what's going on. Scott Glenn, Sam Neill, James Earl Jones. (1990, color, PG, violence, profanity.)

MUTINY ON THE BOUNTY. Classic version of the oft-filmed story pits sailor Clark Gable against Captain Charles Laughton, resulting in mutiny on the high seas. Excellent cast includes Franchot Tone, Donald Crisp, Spring Byington. (1935, black and white, not rated.)

THE SEA HAWK. Errol Flynn is at his swashbuckling best in this first-rate romantic adventure about a buccaneer who goes after a Spanish fleet with his queen's blessing. Great music, sets, and costumes. Brenda Marshall, Flora Robson, Claude Rains, Henry Daniell. (1940, black and white, not rated.)

SWISS FAMILY ROBINSON. A wild ride from Disney, with a shipwrecked family (John Mills, Dorothy McGuire, James MacArthur) making an island their home, then having to deal with pirates. (1960, color, not rated.)

TREASURE ISLAND. Three fine versions of this classic tale are available on video: the earliest, in black and white, with Wallace Beery as Long John Silver and Jackie Cooper as Jim Hawkins; a remake by Disney, in color, with Robert Newton and Bobby Driscoll; and the most recent, made for cable television, with Charlton Heston and Christian Bale. All are quite good, though the latter two are rather violent. (1934/1950/1990, not rated.)

20,000 LEAGUES UNDER THE SEA. First-rate fantasy adventure from Disney, based on the Jules Verne story of Captain Nemo (James Mason) and his underwater ship reluctantly taking on ship-wrecked Kirk Douglas, Paul Lukas, and Peter Lorre. (1954, color, not rated.)

WESTERNS

Westerns seem to be the most difficult genre for young people today to appreciate. Cowpokes sitting tall in the saddle, riding horses, twirling six-shooters, and walking down Main Street to square off against unshaven gunsling-ers—is it any wonder they seem old-fashioned to kids raised on *Star Wars* and *Indiana Jones* movies and Nintendo? Modern audiences seem to prefer that their heroes carry laser guns and fight off tentacled aliens that drool. But there are many great films with a Western motif, and if you pick the right one, you just might convert that hard-nosed youngun' of yours:

THE CLASSICS
...

CIMARRON. Dated, but worth a look for its epic scope, Oklahoma land-rush sequence, and the fact that this is the only traditional Western to ever win the best picture Oscar. Based on Edna Ferber's novel. Richard Dix, Irene Dunne, Estelle Taylor. (1931, black and white, not rated.)

DODGE CITY. Errol Flynn out West, with lots of action as an ex-soldier and trail boss clean up rowdy Kansas before the railroad comes through. Olivia de Havilland, Ann Sheridan, Bruce Cabot. (1939, color, not rated.)

EL DORADO. Sharp and funny performances from the stars give an edge to this comedy-laden yarn about an aging gunslinger (John Wayne) and a drunken sheriff (Robert Mitchum) trying to fend off a range war. James Caan, Arthur Hunnicutt, Edward Asner. (1967, color, not rated.)

THE GUNFIGHTER. Gregory Peck is the gunslinger trying to live down his past in this moody, evocative Western. Karl Malden, Jean Parker. (1950, black and white, not rated.)

HIGH NOON. Gary Cooper stars in this spare Western about a marshall who is deserted by the townfolk as he tries to defend himself against a band of outlaws due to arrive on the noon train. Deceptively simple, with a powerhouse message. Considered by many to be the most perfect Western ever made. (1952, black and white, not rated.)

THE MAGNIFICENT SEVEN. Yul Brynner rounds up six gunfighters (Steve McQueen, James Coburn, and Charles Bronson among them) to help poor Mexican villagers being harassed by Eli Wallach and his gang. (1960, color, not rated.)

THE MAN FROM SNOWY RIVER/RETURN TO SNOWY RIVER. The first is an excellent old-fashioned Western set in Australia, with Tom Burlinson as the stubborn young man who meets his match in the even more stubborn daughter (Sigrid Thornton) of his boss, costarring Jack Thompson and Kirk Douglas (in dual roles). The second is a pleasant followup, with Brian Dennehy costarring. (1982/1988, color, PG, violence, profanity.)

THE NAKED SPUR. Tough character study has James Stewart as an independent bounty hunter, reluctantly strapped with a posse, tracking down killer Robert Ryan, finding that bringing him in won't be easy. Janet Leigh. (1953, color, not rated.)

RIO BRAVO. Terrific tale of sheriff John Wayne trying to keep a killer in jail with help from a band of misfits (Dean Martin, Ricky Nelson, Angie Dickinson, Walter Brennan). (1959, color, not rated.)

SHANE. Classic story of stoic gunfighter staying with a farm family and idolized by a young boy, much to his mother's chagrin. Gorgeous cinematography. Alan Ladd, Jean Arthur, Van Heflin, Jack Palance, Brandon de Wilde. (1953, color, not rated.)

SHENANDOAH. Sentimental, adventuresome look at a Virginia widower (James Stewart) and his family whose lives are changed by the Civil War. Doug McClure, Patrick Wayne, Katharine Ross. (1965, color, not rated.)

John Wayne during his B-movie days, before he made *Stagecoach*.

THEY DIED WITH THEIR BOOTS ON. The story of General George Custer and the events leading up to his "last stand" at Little Big Horn, with Errol Flynn flamboyant as Custer. Olivia de Havilland, Arthur Kennedy, Anthony Quinn, Sydney Greenstreet. (1941, black and white, not rated.)

WESTERN UNION. Robert Young, Randolph Scott, Dean Jagger, and John Carradine headline this look at the laying of the Western Union line in the 1860s, with the usual complications. (1941, color, not rated.)

WINCHESTER '73. James Stewart is a Western Sherlock Holmes here, meticulously tracking down a killer. Shelley Winters, Dan Duryea, Rock Hudson, Tony Curtis. (1950, color, not rated.)

THE FORD FILMS
•••

Director John Ford made many classic Westerns, in

94

Director John Ford, who made many fine Westerns, including *The Man Who Shot Liberty Valance* and *The Searchers.* Photograph taken in Southern Utah. Courtesy *Deseret News.*

addition to movies in other genres, and he filmed the bulk of them in Monument Valley, Utah, after falling in love with the country there while shooting *Stagecoach* in 1939. That film is also of historical note for making a star of John Wayne. These are the best of the Ford legacy:

CHEYENNE AUTUMN. An all-star cast—Richard Widmark, Carroll Baker, Edward G. Robinson, James Stewart—in Ford's final Western, about the Cheyenne Indians returning to their original settlements. (1964, color, not rated.)

FORT APACHE/SHE WORE A YELLOW RIBBON/RIO GRANDE. John Wayne stars in this trio of Ford films, the director's cavalry trilogy. The first costars Henry Fonda and Shirley Temple in the story of a militant commandant (Fonda) about to start a war with the Apaches. (1948, black and white, not rated.) The second has Wayne as an officer about to retire. Joanne Dru costars. (1949, color, not rated.) The third looks at the cavalry after the Civil

War, with Wayne and Maureen O'Hara. (1950, black and white, not rated.)

HOW THE WEST WAS WON. A multichaptered Cinerama film that loses some of its scope on the small screen, but this saga of various personalities who helped shape the West boasts loads of action and an all-star cast, along with three directors, Ford, Henry Hathaway, and George Marshall. George Peppard, Debbie Reynolds, Carroll Baker, James Stewart, Henry Fonda, John Wayne, Gregory Peck. Narrated by Spencer Tracy. (1962, color, not rated.)

THE MAN WHO SHOT LIBERTY VALANCE. One of Ford's best, with Senator James Stewart and his wife (Vera Miles) reminiscing about their early days, back when he was a tenderfoot lawyer from the East and tough cowboy John Wayne tried to help him stand up to evil Lee Marvin. Edmond O'Brien, Lee Van Cleef, John Carradine. (1962, black and white, not rated.)

MY DARLING CLEMENTINE. Classic Ford, a low-key look at Wyatt Earp (Henry Fonda) and Doc Holliday (Victor Mature), leading up to the gunfight at the O.K. Corral. Walter Brennan. (1946, black and white, not rated.)

THE SEARCHERS. Considered by many to be the finest Western ever made, this Ford classic stars John Wayne as an ex-cavalry soldier who reluctantly teams up with a young whippersnapper (Jeffrey Hunter) to track down his niece (Natalie Wood), who's been kidnapped by Indians. Vera Miles. (1956, color, not rated.)

STAGECOACH. This great Ford oater is the movie that made John Wayne a star, casting him as the Ringo Kid, a reluctant gunslinger who helps passengers on a stagecoach journey get through dangerous Indian territory. Claire Trevor, Andy Devine, John Carradine, Thomas Mitchell. (1939, black and white, not rated.)

THREE GODFATHERS. Ford's version of the oft-filmed yarn about three soft-hearted bandits (led by John Wayne) who find a baby in the desert and vow to help it survive. (1948, color, not rated.)

WAGON MASTER. Ward Bond is the title character in this Ford episodic tale of a pair of cowpunchers who link up with a Mormon wagon train headed for Utah in 1879. (1950, black and white, not rated.)

CONTEMPORARY ATTITUDES
...

THE BIG COUNTRY. Former sea captain Gregory Peck and veteran cowhand Charlton Heston square off in this epic Western with two cattle-ranching families warring over water rights. Jean Simmons, Carroll Baker, Burl Ives, Chuck Conners, Charles Bickford. (1958, color, not rated.)

BUTCH CASSIDY AND THE SUNDANCE KID. Paul Newman and Robert Redford are in rare form in this serious yet comic look at the legendary bandits being chased forever by a posse. "Who are those guys?" is still a great line. Katharine Ross, Cloris Leachman. (1969, color, PG, violence, a few profanites.)

THE GREY FOX. Richard Farnsworth shines in the title role as the real-life stagecoach robber Bill Miner, who spent thirty-three years in jail, then found the stagecoach had become obsolete. So, he began robbing trains. (1982, color, PG, violence, profanity.)

JEREMIAH JOHNSON. Robert Redford in perhaps his most famous role as a self-styled mountain man who learns to survive in the wilderness. A gritty, tough study of character and nature. (1972, color, PG, violence, profanity).

THE SHOOTIST. John Wayne's final film, one of his best Westerns, a thoughtful look at a gunfighter dying of cancer who tries to settle his affairs but finds his reputation won't leave him in peace. James Stewart, Lauren Bacall, Ron Howard. (1976, color, PG, violence, profanity.)

SILVERADO. Funny, action-packed Western with some modern sensibilities has Scott Glenn, Kevin Kline, Danny Glover, and Kevin Costner teaming up to take on the bad guys in the title town. John Cleese, Rosanna Arquette, Brian Dennehy, Linda Hunt. (1985, color, PG, violence, profanity.)

WINDWALKER. Before there was *Dances with Wolves,* there was Kieth Merrill's fine look at American Indians, exploring their culture before it was influenced by white settlers. In Cheyenne and Crow, with English subtitles. (1980, PG, violence).

COWPOKE COMEDIES
•••

AN AMERICAN TAIL: FIEVEL GOES WEST. Funny, lush, slam-bang animated sequel, with Fievel and friends heading West, where the Mousekewitz clan hopes to be able to homestead. Voices of James Stewart, Dom DeLuise, John Cleese. (1991, color, G.)

BACK TO THE FUTURE, PART III. Very funny wrap-up to the comic science-fiction film series, with Michael J. Fox and Christopher Lloyd finding themselves in an Old West town, where Fox must prove himself and Lloyd falls in love with schoolmarm Mary Steenburgen. Great fun. (1990, color, PG, violence, profanity).

CALAMITY JANE. Bouncy musical comedy with Doris Day as the title character whose feisty independence is challenged when she falls for Wild Bill Hickock (Howard Keel). (1953, color, not rated.)

CAT BALLOU. Jane Fonda is the title character, but Lee Marvin won his Oscar in the double role of a pathetic, alcoholic gunslinger and his nasty, noseless twin brother. Very funny yarn about a schoolmarm who inadvertantly becomes an outlaw with an inept band of followers. Michael Callan, Dwayne Hickman, Nat King Cole, Stubby Kaye. (1965, color, not rated.)

DESTRY RIDES AGAIN. Riotous Western comedy with James Stewart as pacifist sheriff in wild and woolly town, finding bad guys easier to deal with than rowdy saloon singer Marlene Dietrich. (1939, black and white, not rated.)

THE FRISCO KID. A bit violent in places, but this comedy Western is an enjoyable tale of a Polish rabbi (Gene Wilder) who links up with a young bank robber (Harrison Ford) while crossing the country to San Francisco. (1979, color, PG, violence, profanity.)

GO WEST. The Marx Brothers find themselves in the Old West in this broad comedy, with funny train-chase finale. (1940, black and white, not rated.)

THE HALLELUJAH TRAIL. Enjoyable but overlong comedy Western with Burt Lancaster as a cavalryman taking a shipment of whiskey to Denver while temperance leader Lee Remick tries to stop him. Jim Hutton, Brian Keith, Martin Landau. (1965, color, not rated.)

NORTH TO ALASKA. Funny, fast-paced Western (or "Northern") with John Wayne and Stewart Granger as prospectors with women trouble. Ernie Kovacs, Fabian, Capucine. (1960, color, not rated.)

THE PALEFACE/SON OF PALEFACE. Two of Bob Hope's best films, the first casting him as a meek dentist out West, with Jane Russell as sharpshooting Calamity Jane, and the second with Hope and Roy Rogers competing for bandit Russell's affections. (1948/1952, color, not rated; *The Paleface* was also remade as the 1968 color Don Knotts comedy *The Shakiest Gun in the West.*)

RIDE 'EM COWBOY. Abbott and Costello are on a dude ranch in this farce, laced with some funny routines. Dick Foran, Ella Fitzgerald. (1942, black and white, not rated.)

RUGGLES OF RED GAP/FANCY PANTS. Original comic Western and its remake are both delightful comedies about a staid English butler in the Old West. Charles Laughton and ZaSu Pitts star in the first, Bob Hope and Lucille Ball in the second. (1935, black and white, not rated/1950, color, not rated.)

SUPPORT YOUR LOCAL SHERIFF. James Garner stars in this hilarious spoof of traditional Westerns as a reluctant sheriff in a small town who must deal with local bad guys—but does so in his own, nonviolent way. A riot from start to finish. Joan Hackett, Walter Brennan, Harry Morgan, Jack Elam, Bruce Dern. (1969, color, G.)

THE VILLAIN. Off-the-wall comedy (patterned, believe it or not, after "Road Runner" cartoons) with Kirk Douglas as a bad guy in black trying to set traps for good guy Arnold Schwarzenegger. Ann-Margret, Ruth Buzzi, Paul Lynde, Mel Tillis. (1979, color, PG, comic violence.)

FOR CHILDREN
■ ■

ANIMAL YARNS
■■■

THE ADVENTURES OF MILO AND OTIS. Surprisingly entertaining story of a dog and cat who wander from the farm and experience dangerous adventures together. Cute comic narration by Dudley Moore. (1989, color, G.)

BEETHOVEN. Charles Grodin is exceptional as a hapless suburbanite whose home is invaded by a St. Bernard puppy that grows to huge proportions. The second half of the film, about an evil veterinarian (Dean Jones) is less successful. (1992, color, PG, violence, profanity, vulgarity.)

BENJI/FOR THE LOVE OF BENJI/BENJI THE HUNTED. Delightful series of dog pictures about the lovable pooch getting in and out of various scrapes. (1974/1977/1987, color, G.)

THE BLACK STALLION/THE BLACK STALLION RETURNS. The first is an excellent, stunning tale of a boy lost on an island with the title character, while the second is a more routine story of adventure in the Arabian desert. Kelly Reno stars; Teri Garr is featured in both as his mother. (1979, color, G/1983, color, PG, violence, one profanity.)

BORN FREE/LIVING FREE. The first is an excellent true story about Elsa the lioness, raised in Kenya as a pet and then trained to survive in the wild so she won't be shipped to a zoo. The second is a pretty good follow-up, following Elsa and her three cubs. Virginia McKenna and Bill Travers star in the first; Susan Hampshire and Nigel Davenport in the second. (1966/1972, color, G.)

CASEY'S SHADOW. Walter Matthau is a horse trainer who helps a Cajun family in New Mexico breed a champion in this lightweight but enjoyable film. Alexis Smith. (1978, color, PG, profanity.)

CLARENCE, THE CROSS-EYED LION. The title character becomes a pet when he's taken to an animal behavior clinic in Africa. This film later became the TV series "Daktari." Marshall Thompson, Betsy Drake. (1965, color, not rated.)

FLIPPER/FLIPPER'S NEW ADVENTURE. Cute kids' pictures about young Luke Halpin's relationship with the title dolphin. (1963, color, not rated.)

THE GOLDEN SEAL. A young boy on the Aleutian Islands befriends a rare golden seal and tries to protect it from ruthless hunters. (1983, color, PG, violence, profanity.)

IT'S A DOG'S LIFE. Cute offbeat comedy has a dog telling his life story, from life as a pup in the Bowery to celebrity in a classy dog show. Edmund Gwenn, Dean Jagger. (1955, black and white, not rated.)

LASSIE COME HOME/COURAGE OF LASSIE. Young Elizabeth Taylor stars in these two "Lassie" films, the first about the collie's journey to return to the family that sold her; the second about the dog fighting in World War II and then having to be domesticated again. (1943/1946, color, not rated; also on video is the 1945 *Son of Lassie,* a lesser but fairly enjoyable effort with Peter Lawford.)

MAGIC OF LASSIE. James Stewart and Mickey Rooney star in this remake of *Lassie Come Home,* with songs by Pat and Debby Boone. Alice Faye, Stephanie Zimbalist. (1978, color, not rated.)

NATIONAL VELVET/INTERNATIONAL VELVET. Teen Elizabeth Taylor is wonderful in the first film, yearning to race in England's Grand National Steeplechase (Mickey Rooney and Angela Lansbury costar); the second is a sequel more than thirty years later with Tatum O'Neal as the niece of Taylor's character (played here by Nanette Newman; Anthony Hopkins and Christopher Plummer costar). (1944, color, not rated/1978, color, PG, violence.)

OLD YELLER. Good, sentimental boy-and-his-pooch yarn from Disney, with young Tommy Kirk taking up with a hunting dog. Dorothy McGuire, Fess Parker. (1957, color, not rated.)

WHERE THE RED FERN GROWS. Well-done drama of a boy growing up in 1930s Oklahoma who learns lessons about life while raising

Ethan Hawke with his companion, half-dog, half-wolf, in *White Fang*. ©Buena Vista Pictures Distribution. Used by permission.

a pair of redbone coon hounds. James Whitmore, Beverly Garland, Stewart Peterson. (1974, color, G.)

WHITE FANG. A young man searching for his father's gold mine in Alaska befriends a wolf in this loose adaptation of the Jack London story. A couple of scenes may be a bit too violent for very young ones. (1991, color, PG, violence, profanity.)

THE YEARLING. Enchanting story of a young boy's love for a deer, starring Gregory Peck, Jane Wyman, and young Claude Jarman, Jr. Gorgeous color location photography. (1946, color, not rated.)

ZEBRA IN THE KITCHEN. Jay North (TV's "Dennis the Menace") protests rundown conditions at the local zoo and frees the animals in this cute comedy. Martin Milner, Andy Devine, Joyce Meadows. (1965, color, not rated.)

OUTDOOR ADVENTURES
■■■

THE ADVENTURES OF THE WILDERNESS FAMILY/THE FURTHER AD-VENTURES OF THE WILDERNESS FAMILY/MOUNTAIN FAMILY ROBIN-SON. This trilogy about a family that permanently moves out of the city to the sometimes dangerous Rocky Mountains is a nice blend of wholesome comedy and adventure. Robert F. Logan, Susan Damante Shaw, Buck Flowers. (1975/1978/1979, color, G; the second film in the series is also known as *Wilderness Family, Part 2.*)

AGAINST A CROOKED SKY. A young boy goes after Indians who have kidnapped his sister in this old-fashioned Western, a sort of youth variation on *The Searchers.* Richard Boone, Stewart Peterson. (1975, color, G.)

BAKER'S HAWK. Good family yarn about a young boy who becomes friends with a recluse (Burl Ives) who is being harrassed by vigilantes. Clint Walker, Diane Baker, Lee H. Montgomery. (1976, color, G.)

THE JOURNEY OF NATTY GANN. Fine Disney yarn of a fourteen-year-old girl (Meredith Salenger) during the Depression who rides the rails to look for her father, befriending a wolf along the way. John Cusack. (1985, color, PG, violence.)

SEVEN ALONE. A thirteen-year-old boy leads his six younger brothers and sisters across the wild and woolly terrain of 1840s America as they head West on a two-thousand-mile trek. A true story. Dewey Martin, Aldo Ray, Stewart Peterson. (1975, color, G.)

SHIPWRECKED. This Disney swashbuckler is a rousing throwback to Disney pictures of yore, as a young boy at sea becomes mixed up with ruthless pirates. A delightful surprise. Stian Smestad, Gabriel Byrne, Eva Von Hanno. (1991, color, PG, violence.)

FANTASY/SCIENCE FICTION
■■■

THE ABSENT-MINDED PROFESSOR/SON OF FLUBBER. Winning slapstick fantasies from the Disney folks, with eccentric Fred

Meredith Salenger, left, and John Cusack, right, with untamed wolf in *The Journey of Natty Gann*. ©Buena Vista Pictures Distribution. Used by permission.

MacMurray as the inventor of flubber (flying rubber), which helps his car and local school athletics really take off. Great fun. (1961/1963, black and white, not rated.)

THE ADVENTURES OF MARK TWAIN. Claymation fantasy about Twain with Huck Finn and Becky Thatcher in a flying machine. Fascinating use of clay animation is the highlight. James Whitmore does Twain's voice. (1985, color, G.)

CHITTY CHITTY BANG BANG. OK, overlong children's musical about a flying car, with Dick Van Dyke, Sally Ann Howes. (1968, color, G.)

D.A.R.Y.L. Enjoyable fantasy about a couple adopting a young boy who turns out to be an android. Winning performances by Barret Oliver as the boy and Michael McKean and Mary Beth Hurt as the parents help this one along. (1985, color, PG, violence, pro-fanity.)

DARBY O'GILL AND THE LITTLE PEOPLE. Wonderful Disney fantasy of a tale-spinning old caretaker who can't get anyone to believe him when he comes across the real king of the leprechauns. Sean Connery has a supporting role. (1959, color, not rated.)

DOCTOR DOLITTLE. Musical adaptation of the popular children's books about the title character's relationship with the animal kingdom. Strictly for kids. Rex Harrison, Samantha Eggar, Anthony Newley, Richard Attenborough. (1967, color, not rated.)

THE 5,000 FINGERS OF DR. T. Terrific fantasy conceived by Dr. Seuss has a young boy (Tommy Rettig of TV's "Lassie") dreaming about his cruel piano teacher (Hans Conried), who kidnaps children and forces them to practice. (1953, color, not rated.)

FREAKY FRIDAY. Barbara Harris and Jodie Foster bolster this fantasy of a mother and daughter who find their personalities switched for a day, precursor to a bevy of similar films in the late '80s. John Astin, Patsy Kelly, Dick Van Patten. (1977, color, G.)

HARRY AND THE HENDERSONS. Amusing fantasy has a family on a camping trip running into Bigfoot, literally, then bringing him home and domesticating him. Sweet and silly, like an old Disney film. John Lithgow, Melinda Dillon, Don Ameche. (1987, color, PG, violence, profanity.)

HONEY, I SHRUNK THE KIDS/HONEY, I BLEW UP THE KID. Rick Moranis is the nerdy scientist who performs the title mishaps, with help from Disney special effects. Funny family comedies in the old tradition. (1989/1992, color, PG, violence.)

JACK THE GIANT KILLER. Kerwin Mathews is the title character in this reworking of "Jack and the Beanstalk," battling monsters in the "Sinbad" tradition. (1962, color, not rated.)

THE LAST STARFIGHTER. Light *Star Wars*-style comedy, with Earth teen Lance Guest being recruited for his video-game skills to help a planet under attack. Robert Preston, Dan O'Herlihy. (1984, color, PG, violence, profanity.)

Rick Moranis facing the consequences of his scientific experiment in *Honey, I Shrunk the Kids.* ©Buena Vista Pictures Distribution. Used by permission.

THE LOVE BUG. Very funny Disney slapstick fantasy about a Volkswagen with a mind of its own, starring Dean Jones, Michele Lee, and Buddy Hackett. Far superior to the so-so sequels, *Herbie Rides Again, Herbie Goes to Monte Carlo,* and *Herbie Goes Bananas.* (1969, color, G.)

THE PRINCESS BRIDE. Excellent spoof of swashbuckling fairy tales, framed by Peter Falk giving a lesson on the value of reading books to his young grandson (Fred Savage). Cary Elwes, Mandy Patinkin, Chris Sarandon, Christopher Guest, Andre the Giant, Robin Wright. (1987, color, PG, violence, one profanity.)

THE SHAGGY DOG/THE SHAGGY D.A. Amusing Disney slapstick comedies about hapless Wilby Daniels, who finds a magic ring that turns him into the title character. In the first film, Tommy Kirk is Wilby as a teen, with Fred MacMurray, Annette Funicello, and Roberta Shore in support. The second has Wilby as an adult, played by Dean Jones, with Suzanne Pleshette and Tim Conway in support. (1959, black and white, not rated/1976, color, rated G.)

THE THREE WORLDS OF GULLIVER. Swift's story of a man washed overboard, waking up surrounded by very tiny people in the land of Lilliput, then ending up in Brogdingnag, the land of giants. Great Ray Harryhausen effects enliven this live-action version of the classic tale. Kerwin Mathews. (1960, color, not rated.)

TOM THUMB. Russ Tamblyn is the title character in this lively musical about a tiny woodland youth taken in by a kindly old couple and pursued by rascals (Terry-Thomas, Peter Sellers.) (1958, color, not rated.)

WILLY WONKA AND THE CHOCOLATE FACTORY. Gene Wilder is the title character, a candy maker who takes a group of children on a tour of his factory, with surprising results. Awfully dark in places, though in the end it's an uplifting effort. (1971, color, G.)

MUPPETS
...

THE GREAT MUPPET CAPER. Guest stars galore join in as Kermit and the gang try to solve a London jewel robbery. (1981, color, G.)

THE MUPPET MOVIE. The first movie with Jim Henson's irrepressible Muppets has Kermit leaving his Georgia swamp for Hollywood, running into numerous guest stars. (1979, color, G.)

THE MUPPETS TAKE MANHATTAN. Location photography is a big plus in this bouncy entry, with Kermit and friends trying to put on a Broadway show. Lots of guest stars, of course. (1984, color, G.)

SESAME STREET PRESENTS: FOLLOW THAT BIRD. Big Bird, feeling unwanted, leaves Sesame Street—then gets lonely and tries to hitchhike back. Lots of guest stars (both human and Muppet). (1985, color, G.)

CIRCUS CINEMA
•••

AT THE CIRCUS. Typical Marx Brothers' madness, with Groucho, Chico, and Harpo trying to save a financially strapped circus. Groucho sings "Lydia, the Tatooed Lady." Eve Arden. (1939, black and white, not rated.)

BILLY ROSE'S JUMBO. Rodgers and Hart stage musical, choreographed by Busby Berkeley, with Doris Day as the circus owner's daughter who helps him save the show in 1910. Jimmy Durante, Martha Raye, Stephen Boyd, Dean Jagger. (1962, color, not rated.)

THE CIRCUS. In this inventive slapstick romp, Charlie Chaplin's "Little Tramp" is on the run from the cops when he joins up with a traveling circus and falls for a bareback rider. (1928, black and white, not rated.)

CIRCUS WORLD. John Wayne takes his circus and wild West show on a tour of Europe, while he's also searching for his ex-wife. Rita Hayworth, Claudia Cardinale. (1964, color, not rated.)

THE GREATEST SHOW ON EARTH. Cecil B. DeMille at his overblown, wildly entertaining best, with Betty Hutton as the lovestruck trapeze artist who can't get boss Charlton Heston to give her a second look. Suspense, thrills, and a train wreck finale, with a great cast that includes James Stewart, Dorothy Lamour, Cornel Wilde, and Gloria Graham. (1952, color, not rated.)

TRAPEZE. Aerialist team (Burt Lancaster, Tony Curtis) become more competitive when Gina Lollobrigida attracts both of them. (1956, color, not rated.)

SHIRLEY TEMPLE
•••

THE BLUE BIRD. Two children of a woodcutter look for the bluebird of happiness in a fantasy world. Not altogether satisfying but enjoyable fantasy. (1940, color, not rated.)

CURLY TOP. An orphan, adopted by a playboy, tries to fix him up with her sister. Temple sings "Animal Crackers in My Soup." (1935, black and white, not rated.)

DIMPLES. Temple was at the peak of her childhood form in this pre-Civil War yarn set in the New York Bowery. (1936, black and white, not rated.)

HEIDI. Classic adaptation of the oft-filmed children's story of a young girl being taken from her grandfather. (1937, black and white, not rated.)

LITTLE MISS MARKER. Temple is left as security with a bookie in this Damon Runyon comedy. (1934, black and white, not rated.)

THE LITTLE PRINCESS. Good Temple vehicle set in the Victorian era. When her father goes abroad, she's left in a harsh school but soon wins everyone over. (1939, color, not rated.)

WEE WILLIE WINKIE. One of her best films, with Temple at a British outpost in India where she wins over her gruff grandfather, as well as the rest of the British Army. Victor McLaglen. (1937, black and white, not rated.)

DOMESTIC COMEDIES
∎∎∎

THE PARENT TRAP. Hayley Mills is excellent as twin sisters who meet for the first time when their divorced parents (Maureen O'Hara, Brian Keith) send them to the same summer camp — so they switch places. Great fun. (1961, color, not rated; the three made-for-TV sequels, which followed twenty-five years later, are not on video.)

SAVANNAH SMILES. Popular comedy about a little girl (played by winning Bridgette Andersen) who is accidentally kidnapped by a pair of bungling crooks (Mark Miller, who also wrote the script, and Donovan Scott). Peter Graves, Michael Parks. (1982, color, PG, mild profanity.)

DRAMAS
∎∎∎

JOURNEY FOR MARGARET. Young Margaret O'Brien steals the show in this story of a couple who adopt war orphans. Robert Young, Laraine Day. (1942, black and white, not rated.)

THE SECRET GARDEN. The popular story of an orphan who spruces

109

Walt Disney in 1945. By then he had already made *Fantasia, Pinocchio,* and *Dumbo.* ©Buena Vista Pictures Distribution. Used by permission.

up a mysteriously sealed-off garden on her uncle's estate, a classic film with a fine performance from young Margaret O'Brien. As it begins to bloom, the garden scenes turn to color. (1948, black and white/color, not rated.)

WHERE THE LILIES BLOOM. Four children are orphaned when their father dies, but they keep his death a secret, fearing they'll be separated. Fine family drama. (1973, color, G.)

ANIMATED FEATURES

There are a number of feature-length cartoons available on video besides those made by Walt Disney and Don Bluth; a representative variety is listed in this section.

Though the Disney cartoon features reviewed here are all available in certain video rental stores, after a period of time in the market Disney places its titles on moratorium, or as they now say in the video business, they go "out of print." Therefore, some will not be available for purchase.

Fans may also want to check out animated sequences that appear in certain live-action films:

— Walter Lantz's Oswald the Rabbit appears in the first try at Technicolor animation, which opens the creaky 1930 musical *King of Jazz.*

— Mickey Mouse appears, along with the color Disney cartoon *Hot Chocolate Soldiers,* in the skit film *Hollywood Party* (1934), with Laurel and Hardy, Jimmy Durante, and others.

— Gene Kelly dances with Jerry the Mouse in *Anchors Aweigh* (1944).

— Bugs Bunny and Tweety Pie show up in a dream sequence in the Doris Day film *My Dream Is Yours* (1949).

— There are several imaginative animated sequences in Disney's *So Dear to My Heart* (1945).

— Woody Woodpecker has an appearance in *Destination Moon* (1950).

— Tom and Jerry both join Esther Williams underwater in *Dangerous When Wet* (1953).

— There are well-known animated sequences in Disney's *Mary Poppins* (1965) and *Bedknobs and Broomsticks* (1971).

— Olivia Newton-John becomes a cartoon fish in the pop musical *Xanadu* (1980), courtesy of animator Don Bluth.

— And the 1992 TV spoof *Stay Tuned* has a "RoboCat" sequence by Chuck Jones, in which John Ritter and Pam Dawber become animated mice.

WALT DISNEY
···

ALICE IN WONDERLAND. Riotous adaptation of Lewis Carroll's *Alice*

The fawn Bambi meets the young skunk Flower. ©Buena Vista Pictures Distribution. Used by permission.

in Wonderland and *Through the Looking Glass*. (1951, color, not rated.)

BAMBI. One of the best Disney animated features, with the prince of the forest growing up with Thumper, Flower, and friends. (1951, color, G.)

BEAUTY AND THE BEAST. Fabulous adaptation of the timeless fairy tale, which became the biggest money-making animated feature ever and the first to be nominated for a best picture Oscar. (1991, color, G.)

CINDERELLA. Disney's adaptation of the classic fairy tale is a delight, with a number of winning songs. (1950, color, G.)

DUMBO. Top Disney, the story of the picked-on elephant with the big ears who eventually discovers he can fly. (1941, color, not rated.)

FANTASIA. The one Disney said would never be released on video, superb collection of artistic vignettes set to classical music. (1940, color, G.)

Belle, the Beast, and enchanted rose in *Beauty and the Beast*. ©Buena Vista Pictures Distribution. Used by permission.

THE GREAT MOUSE DETECTIVE. Not Disney's best, but funny and entertaining take on Sherlock Holmes. (1986, color, G.)

THE JUNGLE BOOK. The last animated feature supervised by Disney himself, a funny and tuneful adaptation of Kipling's classic story. (1964, color, G.)

LADY AND THE TRAMP. Wonderful romantic yarn about a proper female cocker spaniel who falls for a stray mutt who likes his freedom. Great fun. (1955, color, G.)

THE LITTLE MERMAID. Supremely popular adaptation of the Hans Christian Andersen tale about a mermaid who falls in love with a human. The film marked a sharp return to form for Disney animators. (1989, color, G.)

101 DALMATIANS. Stylistic animation and lovable characters highlight this story of a couple's pets being dognapped by evil Cruella De Vil. (1961, color, G.)

PETER PAN. One of Disney's best-loved feature cartoons, a funny, bright adaptation of the timeless story of the boy who wouldn't grow up and his battles with Captain Hook. (1953, color, G.)

Dumbo, the famous flying elephant, and his friend, Timothy Mouse. ©Buena Vista Pictures Distribution. Used by permission.

PINOCCHIO. Considered by many critics the pinnacle of Disney's animated features, this adaptation of the Collodi story of a wooden puppet who wants to become a real boy stands as an incredible, timeless work of art and entertainment. (1940, color, G.)

THE RESCUERS/THE RESCUERS DOWN UNDER. Both of these stories of Bernard (voiced by Bob Newhart) and Miss Bianca (Eva Gabor) on assignment for the Rescue Aid Society are delightful adventures. (1977/1990, color, G.)

ROBIN HOOD. Though not up to the usual Disney standard, kids will still enjoy this animated version of the popular characters, here as animals. (1973, color, G.)

SLEEPING BEAUTY. Good adaptation of the fairy tale, with a different animation style for Disney; also the first wide-screen animated film. (1959, color, G.)

THE SWORD IN THE STONE. Popular adaptation of the King Arthur legend, focusing on Arthur as a lad under the tutelage of Merlin the Magician. (1963, color, G.)

DON BLUTH
···

ALL DOGS GO TO HEAVEN. Though too dark for very little ones, this tale of a scalawag mutt who is killed and returns to Earth to redeem himself is a popular item with the younger set. (1989, color, G.)

AN AMERICAN TAIL. Bluth's first teaming with Steven Spielberg was this very good look at an immigrant mouse family coming to America at the turn of the century. (1986, color, G; for sequel, see "Westerns: Cowpoke Comedies.")

THE LAND BEFORE TIME. Delightful tale of dinosaurs on a journey to look for food, meeting up with comic characters along the way. Coproduced by Steven Spielberg. (1988, color, G.)

ROCK-A-DOODLE. An Elvis-style barnyard rooster hits it big as a singer in the city but falls in with bad company, so his old friends leave the farm to bring him back home. The framing story is live action. OK but not Bluth's best work. (1992, color, G.)

THE SECRET OF NIMH. Bluth's first solo film, an underrated visual feast with some wonderful characters, based on the children's book *Mrs. Frisby and the Rats of NIMH.* May be a bit dark for very small children. (1982, color, G.)

"PEANUTS"
···

BON VOYAGE, CHARLIE BROWN (AND DON'T COME BACK). The "Peanuts" kids are exchange students visiting England and France (Snoopy plays at Wimbledon). (1980, color, G.)

A BOY NAMED CHARLIE BROWN. The first feature film based on Charles M. Schulz's "Peanuts" gang, with Charlie Brown being chosen for a national spelling bee. (1969, color, G.)

RACE FOR YOUR LIFE, CHARLIE BROWN. The gang is off to summer camp this time, highlighted by river rafting. (1977, color, G.)

SNOOPY, COME HOME. Snoopy is the focus of this entry in the "Peanuts" series, running into "No Dogs Allowed" signs at every turn. (1972, color, G.)

OTHERS
...

THE BRAVE LITTLE TOASTER. Most enjoyable animated feature about a small band of appliances who leave their wooded home to find their master in the city. (1987, color, not rated)

THE CARE BEARS MOVIE/CARE BEARS MOVIE II: A NEW GENERATION. These two pictures about the sentimental Care-a-Lot bears are strictly for small fry. (1985/1986, color, G.)

CHARLOTTE'S WEB. Very good adaptation of the popular children's novel about the relationship between Wilber the pig, who's sure he'll be tomorrow's bacon, and nurturing Charlotte, a spider in the barn. (1973, color, G.)

THE CHIPMUNK ADVENTURE. OK feature for fans of the Chipmunks, here going around the world in a hot-air balloon race. (1987, color, G.)

FERNGULLY: THE LAST RAINFOREST. Pop musical fairy tale about a rain forest being destroyed, thanks to an evil creature. Environmentally correct cartoon boasts gorgeous animation and Robin Williams as the voice of a loony bat. (1992, color, G.)

GAY PURR-EE. Judy Garland and Robert Goulet do voices for this enjoyable story of a country girl cat in Paris. (1962, color, not rated.)

GULLIVER'S TRAVELS. Max and Dave Fleischer (*Popeye, Betty Boop*) came up with this feature-length cartoon to compete with Disney after *Snow White and the Seven Dwarfs,* and it's a pretty good adaptation of the Swift tale, with a couple of good songs. (1939, color, not rated.)

HEY THERE, IT'S YOGI BEAR. The mischievous bear leaves Jellystone Park and travels cross-country to New York. (1964, color, not rated.)

HOPPITY GOES TO TOWN. Dave Fleischer's follow-up to *Gulliver's Travels* is a cute look at the world from the viewpoint of various bugs, laced with so-so songs. (1941, color, not rated; also known as *Mr. Bug Goes to Town.*)

JETSONS – THE MOVIE. Mediocre feature based on the popular '60s TV series about a futuristic family. (1990, color, G.)

THE MAN CALLED FLINTSTONE. TV's "The Flintstones" made their big-screen debut in this spoof of James Bond and other spy pictures, with Fred resembling agent Rock Slag. (1966, color, not rated.)

THE PHANTOM TOLLBOOTH. Veteran animator Chuck Jones was the guiding light for this sophisticated story of a boy who enters a magical world called the Kingdom of Wisdom. Opens and closes with live-action sequences. (1970, color, G; also known as *The Adventures of Milo in the Phantom Tollbooth.*)

THE POINT. Delightful morality tale of young boy banished from the kingdom of pointy-headed people because his head is round. Narrated by Ringo Starr. Made for TV. (1971, color, not rated.)

TINY TOONS ADVENTURES: HOW I SPENT MY VACATION. Superior Steven Spielberg-produced animated feature (made for video), based on the "Tiny Toons" TV series, with plenty of zippy one-liners for parents as well as slapstick for the kids. (1992, color, G.)

YELLOW SUBMARINE. Based on a number of Beatles songs, this wild, highly imaginative animated feature has John, Paul, George, and Ringo saving Pepperland from the Blue Meanies. (1968, color, G.)

LIVE ACTION WITH ANIMATION
...

THE INCREDIBLE MR. LIMPET. Don Knotts can't get into the Navy during World War II, but when he's transformed into an animated fish he gets to help the war effort. Enjoyable live-action/animation kids' stuff. (1962, color, not rated.)

PETE'S DRAGON. Animated dragon befriends an orphaned young boy in this kids' fantasy. OK but too long. Helen Reddy, Jim Dale, Mickey Rooney, Red Buttons, Shelley Winters. (1977, color, G.)

WHO FRAMED ROGER RABBIT. Though it's a bit too sophisticated in places (and has some unnecessary vulgar jokes), this fast and funny blend of live-action and animation set a new standard for the process. The highlights are detective Bob Hoskins's journey through Toon Town and the climactic moment when every cartoon character you can imagine shows up. Steven Spielberg co-produced with Disney. (1988, color, PG, violence, vulgarity.)

SCIENCE FICTION AND FANTASY

SCIENCE FICTION
...

BACK TO THE FUTURE. The most enjoyable (and profitable) of the trilogy is this first effort, with Michael J. Fox time-traveling to the past where he meets his own parents in high school. Christopher Lloyd, Lea Thompson. (1985, color, PG, violence, profanity; forget the first sequel; for *Part 3,* see "Westerns: Cowpoke Comedies.")

CLOSE ENCOUNTERS OF THE THIRD KIND. Steven Spielberg's magical classic about communication with space aliens and the way an ordinary guy (Richard Dreyfuss) becomes obsessed with making contact. Francois Truffaut, Melinda Dillon, Teri Garr. (1977, color, PG, violence, profanity.)

E.T. THE EXTRA-TERRESTRIAL. The most popular film of all time, according to box-office receipts, a most enjoyable fantasy with a young boy befriending a lost little alien. Steven Spielberg at the peak of his powers. Dee Wallace, Henry Thomas, Peter Coyote, Drew Barrymore. (1982, color, PG, violence, a couple of profanities.)

FORBIDDEN PLANET. A real trendsetter, this science fiction thriller has Leslie Nielsen and crew landing on a remote planet to discover that the only inhabitants left are a mad scientist (Walter Pidgeon) and his daughter (Anne Francis). Nice blend of science fiction, horror, and comedy—and Robby the Robot, of course. Based on Shakespeare's *The Tempest,* believe it or not. (1956, color, not rated.)

Bill Campbell in *The Rocketeer*. ©Buena Vista Pictures Distribution. Used by permission.

I MARRIED A MONSTER FROM OUTER SPACE. Despite the ridiculous title, this is a pretty good reworking of *Invasion of the Body Snatchers,* with new bride Gloria Talbott discovering secrets about her husband, Tom Tryon. (1958, black and white, not rated.)

INVASION OF THE BODY SNATCHERS. The classic original is the preferred version, with Kevin McCarthy relating a wild story to authorities of insidious pods from outer space taking over the human population one by one. Dana Wynter, Carolyn Jones. (1956, black and white, not rated.)

LATE FOR DINNER. Interesting time-travel melodrama about two young men in 1962 who find themselves in a cryogenics experiment and awaken thirty years later. (1991, color, PG, violence, profanity.)

THE ROCKETEER. Entertaining comic tale of young '30s stunt pilot who finds a rocket jetpack invented by Howard Hughes and uses it to battle Nazis. May be too violent for young children. (1991, color, PG, violence, profanity, vulgarity.)

THE THING (FROM ANOTHER WORLD). This classic science fiction horror yarn (with liberal doses of comedy) is extremely chilling (and chilly), with a quick-paced story of a remote Arctic outpost where a nasty-tempered alien crashes his saucer, is frozen in the ice, and accidentally thaws. Forget the gory, R-rated 1982 remake. (1951, black and white, not rated.)

WAR OF THE WORLDS. Great special effects and a strong, intelligent narrative of Martians attacking the earth make George Pal's adaptation of the H. G. Wells story a superior effort. Gene Barry stars; narrated by Cedric Hardwicke. (1953, color, not rated.)

WESTWORLD. Wild yarn about an adult vacation resort at which people indulge their fantasies with humanoid robots in historical period settings, until the robots malfunction and start killing the guests. Yul Brynner, as a gunslinger robot (spoofing his *Magnificent Seven* role), steals the show. Richard Benjamin, James Brolin. (1973, color, PG, violence, profanity; the 1976 sequel, *Futureworld,* isn't bad either.)

FANTASIES
...

THE DAY OF THE DOLPHIN. George C. Scott stars in this fantasy of dolphins being used in a plot to assassinate the president, sort of "Flipper as James Bond." Enjoyable fluff. (1973, color, PG, violence, profanity.)

JOURNEY TO THE CENTER OF THE EARTH. Jules Verne's story gets glossy film treatment here as James Mason and a small band go off to mysterious adventures. Most enjoyable fantasy. Pat Boone, Arlene Dahl. (1959, color, not rated.)

LOST HORIZON. Frank Capra's classic version of the James Hilton novel about survivors of a plane crash in the Himalayas who stumble upon the magical world of Shangri-la. Great filmmaking, with Ronald Colman, Jane Wyatt, Edward Everett Horton, Sam Jaffe. (1937, black and white, not rated.)

THE NEVERENDING STORY/THE NEVERENDING STORY II: THE NEXT CHAPTER. Well-made films about the land of Fantasia, filled with strange creatures, with a message to youngsters about the importance of reading. The first film is better than the second, however. The second includes *Box Office Bunny,* a fresh Bugs Bunny cartoon. (1984/1990, color, PG, violence.)

THE THIEF OF BAGDAD. The classic Arabian Nights yarn is still an eye-popping spectacle in the two versions recommended here, the first a silent classic with Douglas Fairbanks and the second a lavish British production starring Sabu. (1924, black and white, not rated/1940, color, not rated.)

MYSTERIES/THRILLERS

AND THEN THERE WERE NONE. Agatha Christie's memorable murder mystery about ten people summoned to a remote island where one of them kills the others one by one. Barry Fitzgerald, Walter Huston, Louis Hayward, Roland Young. (1945, black and white, not rated; forget the awful remakes, titled *Ten Little Indians.*)

THE BIG SLEEP. Humphrey Bogart and Lauren Bacall star in this supremely entertaining Philip Marlow mystery, loaded with clever dialogue. Cowritten by William Faulkner. (1946, black and white, not rated.)

THE HOUND OF THE BASKERVILLES/THE ADVENTURES OF SHERLOCK HOLMES. These Holmes-Watson yarns, the first two starring Basil Rathbone and Nigel Bruce, are by far the best. Both are period pieces rich in atmosphere, thrills, and characterization, (1939/1939, black and white, not rated; the 1959 color version of *The Hound of the Baskervilles,* with Peter Cushing and Christopher Lee, is also good, though more of a horror movie.)

THE MALTESE FALCON. One of the best mysteries ever, John Huston's first directing effort, with Humphrey Bogart as Philip Marlowe ducking crosses and double crosses at every turn as he investigates his partner's murder. Mary Astor, Peter Lorre, Sydney Greenstreet. (1941, black and white, not rated.)

Humphrey Bogart in *The Maltese Falcon*. ©1941 Turner Entertainment Company. All rights reserved. Used by permission.

MURDER, SHE SAID/MURDER AT THE GALLOP/MURDER AHOY/MURDER MOST FOUL. Four splendid little murder mysteries based on Agatha Christie stories and starring Margaret Rutherford as Miss Marple. Funny and clever. (1961/1963/1964/1965, black and white, not rated.)

OUT OF THE PAST. Excellent film noir with Robert Mitchum as a small-town gas station attendant who can't shake his past with gangster Kirk Douglas. One of the great '40s cross and double-cross thrillers. Jane Greer, Rhonda Fleming. (1947, black and white, not rated.)

SLEUTH. The ultimate game of one-upmanship is played in this terrific comic thriller, with a pair of knockout performances: Laurence Olivier, as a mystery writer, invites Michael Caine in for some surprises—and is surprised himself. (1972, color, PG, violence, profanity.)

WITNESS FOR THE PROSECUTION. Classic Agatha Christie murder mystery mixes drama and humor as Tyrone Power is put on trial in London for the murder of a wealthy widow—and his wife (Marlene Dietrich) is set to testify against him. Charles Laughton is great as Power's defense attorney, as is Elsa Lanchester as Laughton's fussy nurse. (1957, black and white, not rated.)

ALFRED HITCHCOCK
■■■

FOREIGN CORRESPONDENT. Hitchcock's thriller about a reporter on the trail of a kidnapped diplomat, with Joel McCrea and Laraine Day. (1940, black and white, not rated.)

THE LADY VANISHES. Michael Redgrave and Margaret Lockwood try to find out why an old woman (Dame May Whitty) has disappeared from a train in this perfect mix of comedy and mystery. (1938, black and white, not rated.)

THE MAN WHO KNEW TOO MUCH. Two versions are available of this thriller about an American couple inadvertently thrown into international intrigue, both directed by Hitchcock. The first, with Leslie Banks and Edna Best, is considered by critics the best, but the general public leans toward the remake with James Stewart and Doris Day. (1934, black and white, not rated/1956, color, not rated.)

NORTH BY NORTHWEST. Cary Grant is Hitchcock's quintessential innocent man on the run in this colorful, exciting yarn, winding up on Mount Rushmore. James Mason, Eva Marie Saint, Martin Landau. (1959, color, not rated.)

REAR WINDOW. Photographer James Stewart spies on his tenement neighbors while laid up with a broken leg and witnesses a murder. Glossy romantic thriller, with added bonus of Grace Kelly and Thelma Ritter engaging in witty repartee with Stewart. Wendell Corey, Raymond Burr. (1954, color, not rated.)

SABOTEUR. Prime Hitchcock, with Robert Cummings as a defense plant worker pursued by Nazi agents across America, with a harrowing climax atop the Statue of Liberty. Priscilla Lane. (1942, black and white, not rated.)

Cary Grant and Eva Marie Saint in *North by Northwest*. ©1959 Turner Entertainment Company. All rights reserved. Used by permission.

SHADOW OF A DOUBT. A young woman (Teresa Wright) begins to suspect her Uncle Charly (Joseph Cotten) may be a notorious murderer in this mix of mystery and small-town Americana, expertly blended by Hitchcock. MacDonald Carey, Hume Cronyn. (1943, black and white, not rated.)

STRANGERS ON A TRAIN. Tennis pro Farley Granger, who's having trouble with his estranged wife, is approached by Robert Walker, who suggests swapping murders. Granger doesn't take it seriously — until his wife is killed. Hitchcock in his prime, with ultra-tense merry-go-round climax. (1951, black and white, not rated.)

THE 39 STEPS. The prototype for Hitchcock's later work, with Robert Donat as an innocent pulled into a spy ring, taking it on the lam and linking up with Madeleine Carroll. (1935, black and white, not rated.)

HITCHCOCK WANNABES
■■■

ARABESQUE. College professor Gregory Peck on the run while tangling with spies, with Sophia Loren along for the ride. (1966, color, not rated.)

CHARADE. Cary Grant and Audrey Hepburn are a wonderful team in this comedy thriller about a widow being wooed by a mystery man as she is terrorized by thugs (James Coburn, George Kennedy). Walter Matthau. (1963, color, not rated.)

CRACK-UP. Respected art critic Pat O'Brien stumbles onto an art-forgery ring and becomes a Hitchcock-style innocent man on the run. Claire Trevor. (1946, black and white, not rated.)

THE PRIZE. Paul Newman stars in this glossy yarn about spies terrorizing a Nobel Prize winner (Edward G. Robinson) in Stockholm. Elke Sommer, Diane Baker. (1963, color, not rated.)

SPORTS MOVIES

BASEBALL

BANG THE DRUM SLOWLY. Robert De Niro is the simple-minded catcher dying of Hodgkin's disease, and Michael Moriarty is the vibrant pitcher who befriends him in this stirring drama. (1972, color, PG, profanity; also available is a black-and-white 1956 TV version, starring Paul Newman.)

BLUE SKIES AGAIN. Amusing comedy-drama about a young woman (Robyn Barto) who aspires to be the first female player in the major leagues. Harry Hamlin, Mimi Rogers. (1983, color, PG, profanity.)

DAMN YANKEES. Faithful translation of the musical stage hit about an old man who regains his youth and becomes a baseball star after making a pact with the devil. Terrific songs and two great performances—Gwen Verdon as Lola and Ray Walston as Applegate. Tab Hunter is so-so in the lead. (1958, color, not rated.)

FEAR STRIKES OUT. Anthony Perkins and Karl Malden are very good as Jimmy Piersall and his overbearing father, respectively, in this story of the Boston Red Sox player who overcame mental illness. (1957, black and white, not rated.)

FIELD OF DREAMS. Excellent Frank Capra-style fantasy about reconciling with loved ones, as an Iowa farmer hears a mysterious voice telling him to build a baseball diamond in his cornfield. (1989, color, PG, profanity).

THE JACKIE ROBINSON STORY/THE COURT-MARTIAL OF JACKIE ROBINSON. The first is a biographical film starring Robinson himself, and the second is a TV-movie about his run-ins with racism in the service. Both are quite good. Ruby Dee plays Robinson's wife in the first film and his mother in the second. (1950, black and white, not rated/1990, color, not rated.)

THE PRIDE OF ST. LOUIS. Sentimental biography of baseball star and all-around character Dizzy Dean (played well by Dan Dailey). (1952, black and white, not rated.)

THE PRIDE OF THE YANKEES. Gary Cooper is very good as Lou Gehrig in this excellent weepy biography, with great support from Teresa Wright, Walter Brennan, Dan Duryea, and Babe Ruth (as himself). (1942, black and white, not rated.)

TAKE ME OUT TO THE BALL GAME. Gene Kelly and Frank Sinatra are a delightful pair of baseball players in this light Busby Berkeley musical-comedy, with Esther Williams as the team's owner. (1949, color, not rated.)

FOOTBALL
...

BRIAN'S SONG. Excellent made-for-TV drama about friendship of Chicago Bears teammates Brian Piccolo and Gale Sayers, played superbly by James Caan and Billy Dee Williams, respectively. (1970, color, G.)

JIM THORPE – ALL AMERICAN. The ups and downs of the American Indian athlete who won gold medals in the 1912 Olympics, only to lose them because he had played semipro baseball, then going on to pro baseball and football careers. Burt Lancaster stars. (1951, black and white, not rated.)

KNUTE ROCKNE – ALL AMERICAN. Pat O'Brien is the famed Notre Dame football coach, and Ronald Reagan is star player George Gipp. O'Brien is excellent. (1940, black and white, not rated.)

OTHER SPORTS
...

THE CHAMP. There are two versions of this sentimental weeper, the story of an over-the-hill boxer and his devotion to his young son: the first a classic with Wallace Beery (who won an Oscar) and Jackie Cooper, the second a so-so remake with Jon Voight and Ricky Schroeder. Obviously, the first is the winner. (1931, black and white, not rated/1979, color, PG, violence, profanity; also remade as the 1953 black-and-white drama *The Clown,* with Red Skelton and Tim Considine.)

CHARIOTS OF FIRE. Oscar-winning true story of two disparate runners in the 1924 Olympics who are equally driven. A wonderful, emotionally satisfying character study. Ben Cross, Ian Charleson, John Gielgud. (1981, color, PG, profanity.)

HOOSIERS. Rousing look at small-town Indiana basketball team, pulled together by a coach who needs a shot of self-esteem. Gene Hackman is great as the coach, as are Barbara Hershey and Dennis Hopper. (1986, color, PG, on-court violence, mild profanity.)

ICE CASTLES. Young ice skater (Lynn-Holly Johnson) is blinded in an accident, cutting her Olympic potential short in this teary melodrama. Well-acted by Johnson, Robby Benson, Colleen Dewhurst, Tom Skerritt. (1979, color, PG, profanity.)

PHAR LAP. Uplifting true story of champion Australian racehorse and the stableboy (Tom Burlinson of *The Man from Snowy River*) who believed in him. Ron Leibman. (1983, color, PG, profanity.)

WAR/MILITARY PICTURES

ACTION
...

THE AFRICAN QUEEN. One of the all-time great comic adventures, as a boozy trader (Humphrey Bogart, who won an Oscar) takes a prim missionary (Katharine Hepburn) down the Congo in 1915 during World War I. Robert Morley, Theodore Bikel; directed by John Huston. (1951, color, not rated.)

THE BRIDGE ON THE RIVER KWAI. Spectacular David Lean epic has a colonel (Alec Guinness) pushing his men in a Japanese POW camp to build a bridge as a way of showing British superiority, but an American officer (William Holden) plots to blow it up. Great filmmaking. Jack Hawkins, Sessue Hayakawa. Two tapes. (1957, color, not rated.)

THE GREAT ESCAPE. All-star cast in an exciting true story—in a massive effort, Allied soldiers escape from a German POW camp. Steve McQueen, James Garner, Richard Attenborough, Charles Bronson, James Coburn. (1963, color, not rated.)

RUN SILENT, RUN DEEP. Submarine commander (Clark Gable) clashes with his lieutenant (Burt Lancaster) in this tense World War II drama. Jack Warden, Don Rickles. (1958, black and white, not rated.)

COMEDIES
...

FATHER GOOSE. Cary Grant is a cranky beachcomber during World War II who finds himself straddled with teacher Leslie Caron and her seven young schoolgirls. (1964, color, not rated.)

HAIL THE CONQUERING HERO. A visual and verbal comic feast from Preston Sturges, about a 4-F young man thought to be a Marine wartime hero when he returns home. Riotous performances from Eddie Bracken, William Demarest, and Franklin Pangborn. (1944, black and white, not rated.)

NO TIME FOR SERGEANTS. This hilarious service comedy made a star of Andy Griffith, who repeats his stage role as a country rube inducted into the service. Don Knotts has a funny bit as a psychiatrist. (1958, black and white, not rated; also available is a black-and-white 1955 TV version, also starring Griffith.)

A SOUTHERN YANKEE. Arguably Red Skelton's best movie, a Civil War farce loaded with great gags conceived by an uncredited Buster Keaton. Arlene Dahl, Brian Donlevy. (1948, black and white, not rated.)

STALAG 17. An excellent World War II comedy drama about POWs in a German camp, with William Holden (who won an Oscar) as an American sergeant whose cynicism makes him the chief suspect when evidence of a spy is uncovered. Otto Preminger, Robert Strauss, Harvey Lembeck, Peter Graves. (1953, black and white, not rated.)

DRAMAS
...

THE BEST YEARS OF OUR LIVES. Great story of World War II veterans returning home, focusing on Fredric March, Dana Andrews, and Harold Russell. Excellent in every respect. Myrna Loy, Teresa Wright. (1946, black and white, not rated.)

CADENCE. Sincere, if uneven look at an Army private (Charlie Sheen) thrown into the stockade on a West German post in 1965, having to deal with wary black inmates and a psychotic sergeant (Martin Sheen, who also directed). Larry Fishburne, Ramon Estevez, F. Murray Abraham. (1991, color, PG, violence, profanity.)

CASABLANCA. One of the greatest romantic melodramas of all time, with terrific dialogue, a great story revolving around World War II, and a perfect cast, headed by Humphrey Bogart and Ingrid Bergman. (1942, black and white, not rated.)

THE DIARY OF ANNE FRANK. Very good adaptation of the stage play, the true story of Jewish refugees hiding in a factory attic in Amsterdam. Excellent performances from Millie Perkins, Joseph Schildkraut, Shelley Winters, Richard Beymer, Lou Jacobi, Diane Baker, and Ed Wynn. (1959, black and white, not rated.)

JUDGMENT AT NUREMBERG. Excellent historical drama with Spencer Tracy as the American judge who must preside over war-crime trials after World War II. Burt Lancaster, Richard Widmark, Marlene Dietrich, Judy Garland, Maximilian Schell, Montgomery Clift, William Shatner. (1961, black and white, not rated.)

MRS. MINIVER. Wartime propaganda at its best, with Greer Garson in the title role as a British wife/mother holding the family together through the ravages of World War II. Won seven Oscars. (1942, black and white, not rated.)

Humphrey Bogart and Ingrid Bergman in *Casablanca*. ©1943 Turner Entertainment Company. All rights reserved. Used by permission.

THE RED BADGE OF COURAGE. John Huston directed this excellent adaptation of Stephen Crane's novel, with Audie Murphy as the soldier who runs from battle during the Civil War. (1951, black and white, not rated.)

SERGEANT YORK. True story of pacifist who became a World War I hero. Features a mesmerizing, Oscar-winning central performance by Gary Cooper. Walter Brennan. (1941, black and white, not rated.)

SINCE YOU WENT AWAY. In this stateside melodrama, Claudette Colbert heads the family while her husband is off fighting World War II. Bolstered by a fine cast: Jennifer Jones, Joseph Cotten, Shirley Temple, Monty Woolley, Agnes Moorehead, Hattie McDaniel, Keenan Wynn, Robert Walker, Lionel Barrymore. (1944, black and white, not rated.)

TOMORROW IS FOREVER. Very good soap opera has Claudette Colbert remarrying when her husband (Orson Welles) is listed as a casualty of World War II. The kicker, of course, is that he's not dead. Young Natalie Wood plays his adopted daughter. (1946, black and white, not rated.)

130

Gary Cooper in *Sergeant York*. ©1941 Turner Entertainment Company. All rights reserved. Used by permission.

TWELVE O'CLOCK HIGH. Thoughtful wartime drama with Gregory Peck as a flight commander in England getting involved with his flyers' personal lives. Hugh Marlowe, Gary Merrill, Dean Jagger (who won an Oscar). (1949, black and white, not rated.)

HALLOWEEN MOVIES/HORROR

When Halloween rolls around, the phones ring off the hook as people ask about something they can watch that is scary but not gory. This is true especially for parents who are looking for a chiller they can share with the kids. It's a hard call because, of all the movie genres, horror is the one that has gone to seed in the worst way over the past couple of decades. Personally, I prefer a good screen

131

scare to being grossed out, but most horror movies today go for the easy shock, which usually involves buckets of blood or some other form of glop-and-goo special effects. So, you won't find the *Halloween* or *Nightmare on Elm Street* or *Friday the 13th* movies here.

But that still doesn't mean the following recommendations are movies for very young children. All horror movies show death in one form or another, and many deal with supernatural circumstances. (And some listed below carry a warning that they are especially intense or violent, despite being much less explicit than most modern-day horror.)

Of course, some kids will be too frightened by anything that is tense or scary. Even the Abbott and Costello monster comedies can be too harsh in some cases. So, some caution is suggested here. But for older children and adults, the ones listed in this section are all pretty safe choices.

I might mention that quite a few science-fiction movies also make great Halloween viewing because of their monsters and planet-in-dire-peril scenes. *Forbidden Planet, I Married a Monster from Outer Space, Invasion of the Body Snatchers, The Thing (from Another World), War of the Worlds,* and *Westworld* are six of the best. The "Science Fiction" section contains descriptions of these films.

VAMPIRES
···

DRACULA. The original Bela Lugosi version is slow and a bit hokey by today's standards, but fans of oldies will enjoy seeing Lugosi recreate his Broadway role in what is still the standard interpretation of the character. The made-for-TV version, with Jack Palance, is better than you might think, with Palance really sinking his teeth into the role, so to speak. (1931, black and white, not rated/1973, color, not rated.)

HORROR OF DRACULA. This British production from Hammer Films was Christopher Lee's first outing as the count, with Peter Cushing as Van Helsing. Colorful, made with flourish and broad

Bela Lugosi, who starred in such vintage horror movies as *Dracula* and *The Black Cat*.

performances, introducing sex and gore to mainstream horror movies (though still in PG territory by today's standards). Followed by six sequels, though only the inferior 1960 *Brides of Dracula* is on video. (1958, color, not rated.)

THE NIGHT STALKER. Made-for-TV horror, with liberal doses of comedy, as wise guy Las Vegas reporter Darren McGavin encounters a vampire—but, of course, no one believes him. Carol Lynley. (1971, color, not rated.)

NOSFERATU. The first Dracula movie, a German silent production

133

that fans of silent cinema will enjoy. (1922, black and white, not rated; the 1979 Werner Herzog remake is not on video.)

SALEM'S LOT. One of the better Stephen King adaptations. This made-for-TV yarn about a writer (David Soul) who discovers a vampire living in a small Maine community packs a solid, very scary punch. James Mason, Bonnie Bedelia. (1979, color, PG, violence.)

FRANKENSTEIN
•••

BRIDE OF FRANKENSTEIN. Considered by many critics the best of the Universal horror films, this sequel to *Frankenstein* has the good doctor meeting up with an even crazier scientist and ultimately creating a horrifying mate (Elsa Lanchester) for Dr. Frankenstein's monster (Boris Karloff). (1935, black and white, not rated.)

THE CURSE OF FRANKENSTEIN. The first of Hammer Film's string of color horror remakes, pumping up the blood and sex (though definitely in what would be PG territory today). Peter Cushing is excellent as the good doctor; Christopher Lee is the monster. Followed by six sequels, but only one (the disappointing *Evil of Frankenstein*) is on video. (1957, color, not rated.)

FRANKENSTEIN. The original shocker, with Boris Karloff as the monster, made him a star and began a cycle of horror movies from Universal Pictures. This one seems rather ancient today, but it is still enjoyable on its own terms. (1931, black and white, not rated.)

FRANKENSTEIN MEETS THE WOLF MAN. This outing in the series is enjoyable more for camp value than for real scares, especially the final one-on-one battle between Frankenstein's monster (Bela Lugosi) and the Wolf Man (Lon Chaney, Jr.). Still fun, though. (1943, black and white, not rated.)

SON OF FRANKENSTEIN. Third in the series features Boris Karloff as the monster (for the last time), revived by the late doctor's son (Basil Rathbone), with help from the demented hunchback Ygor (Bela Lugosi). Very well made. (1939, black and white, not rated.)

WEREWOLVES
■■■

WEREWOLF OF LONDON. Henry Hull is the botanist who discovers his fate after being bitten by a wolf in this chiller, the first werewolf movie. Not quite up to the later *The Wolf Man,* however. (1935, black and white, not rated.)

THE WOLF MAN. Lon Chaney, Jr., was so good in this story of an innocent young man who is bitten by a werewolf that he was identified with the role for the rest of his life (and he repeated it many times in subsequent Universal films). One of the best of the Universal horror films. Claude Rains, Ralph Bellamy, Bela Lugosi. (1941, black and white, not rated.)

GHOST STORIES
■■■

THE HAUNTING. One of the best, most frightening haunted house movies ever, with Julie Harris among a group of innocents who sleep over—and wish they'd stayed home instead. Based on Shirley Jackson's equally frightening novel, *The Haunting of Hill House.* (1963, black and white, not rated.)

POLTERGEIST. Steven Spielberg's clever, funny, and very scary haunted-house-in-suburbia tale, with a first-rate cast and dazzling special effects. Definitely not for young children, however. Craig T. Nelson, JoBeth Williams. Followed by two inferior sequels. (1982, color, PG, violence, profanity).

THE UNINVITED. Spooky ghost yarn with Ray Milland and Ruth Hussey as brother and sister, moving into a haunted house. Effective atmosphere and straightforward storytelling make this one a most superior effort. (1944, black and white, not rated.)

ALFRED HITCHCOCK
■■■

THE BIRDS. Hitchcock's terrifying tale of our feathered friends turning against us. Deliberately builds up slowly, then really packs a punch. A couple of gory moments; this one is not for young children. (1963, color, not rated.)

PSYCHO. After all these years, Hitchcock's original is still one of the best shockers of all time, with the notorious shower scene a horrifying highlight, as well as that knockout ending. Anthony Perkins, Janet Leigh, Martin Balsam, John Gavin. Followed by three hard R-rated sequels, none of them equal to this one. Not for young children. (1960, black and white, not rated.)

VINCENT PRICE
∎∎∎

THE FLY. This is the tension-filled original, of course, with a scientist (David Hedison) accidentally switching his own head and arm with that of a housefly. Builds deliberately, with a very famous ending. Price is the best friend who tries to help. Skip the gory 1986 remake. (1959, color, not rated.)

HOUSE OF USHER. The best of Roger Corman's eight Edgar Allan Poe adaptations, this lavish tale of madness and murder also features one of Price's best performances. Very scary. (1960, color, not rated.)

THE HOUSE ON THE HAUNTED HILL. Campy William Castle thriller has Price as a millionaire who offers $50,000 each to people who will spend a night in his haunted house. More amusing than scary these days. (1958, black and white, not rated.)

THE MASQUE OF THE RED DEATH. More Corman-Poe, one of his most stylish, thoughtful productions, with Death making an appearance at a lavish ball being thrown by evil Prince Prospero (Price). Forget Corman's 1989 R-rated remake. (1964, color, not rated.)

THE PIT AND THE PENDULUM. Another fine Edgar Allan Poe adaptation by Roger Corman, set after the Spanish Inquisition, with Price as a wacko who begins to believe he's really his father, one of the most notorious torturers of the period. (1961, color, not rated.)

TALES OF TERROR. Price teams up with Peter Lorre and Basil Rathbone for this Roger Corman anthology of four Poe yarns (told in three stories). Price is in all three. The best is *The Black Cat,* with Lorre getting revenge on his cheating wife. (1962, color, not rated.)

TOMB OF LIGEIA. This Corman-Poe adaptation has widowed Price remarrying but being unable to forget his first wife — she won't let him. Another chilling entry. (1965, color, not rated.)

TWICE-TOLD TALES. A Nathaniel Hawthorne anthology, three stories starring Price. This one is a bit slow and overlong, but still offers some effective moments. (1963, color, not rated.)

ANTHOLOGIES
···

ASYLUM. A British film, with four puzzling tales of terror related to psychiatrist Peter Cushing in the institution where he is applying for work, complete with twist ending. Richard Todd, Herbert Lom, Patrick Magee. (1972, color, rated PG, violence.)

THE BLACK CAT/THE RAVEN. These are actually two different hour-long movies first released on one tape (they were recently released again, separately), both starring Boris Karloff and Bela Lugosi. The first film is the best, with Lugosi as a good doctor, trying to reason with devil-worshiper Karloff. The second (not to be confused with the horror comedy of the same name, which also stars Karloff) has mad scientist Lugosi promising a new face to scarred criminal Karloff if he'll help him with dirty deeds (including a "Pit and the Pendulum" climax). (1934/1936, black and white, not rated.)

DEAD OF NIGHT. Michael Redgrave's ventriloquist segment is the best of this excellent anthology, with several intriguing stories about recurring dreams. (1945, black and white, not rated.)

DR. TERROR'S HOUSE OF HORRORS. Peter Cushing is a doctor who tells the fortunes of five men on a train in this enjoyable horror fantasy. Christopher Lee, Michael Gough, Donald Sutherland. (1965, color, not rated.)

FROM BEYOND THE GRAVE. Peter Cushing is the one who tells the stories in this one, as an antique shop owner. Donald Pleasence, David Warner, Lesley-Anne Down. (1973, color, rated PG, violence.)

THE HOUSE THAT DRIPPED BLOOD. Peter Cushing and Christopher Lee also star in this one, set in a haunted house where a Scotland

Yard inspector is told four stories by mysterious residents. Denholm Elliott. (1971, color, PG, violence.)

TALES FROM THE CRYPT. The old British horror movie, not the '80s and '90s cable TV shows. Five yarns related by a sinister monk to people lost in catacombs. From E. C. Comics stories. Peter Cushing, Joan Collins, Ralph Richardson, Richard Greene, Patrick Magee. (1972, color, PG, violence.)

TRILOGY OF TERROR. Karen Black has four roles in three short stories in this made-for-TV horror yarn. The best, about an evil doll, is saved for last. The third is too scary for young children. Gregory Harrison. (1975, color, not rated.)

VAULT OF HORROR. Sequel to *Tales from the Crypt,* with five men trapped in a skyscraper basement, telling each other of their recurring dreams. Terry-Thomas, Glynis Johns, Curt Jurgens, Denholm Elliott. (1973, color, PG, violence.)

MISCELLANEOUS MONSTERS
•••

THE BLOB. The campy original, with young Steve McQueen as a teen who can't convince anyone in town that a killer glob of goo from outer space is eating his neighbors. Goofy fun. Forget the idiotic 1972 sequel and the gory, R-rated 1988 remake. (1956, color, not rated.)

CARNIVAL OF SOULS. Bizarre, low-budget thriller about a woman who is haunted by visions of zombies after she nearly drowns. Loads of atmosphere, with an unexpected ending, this film has developed quite a cult following since its rediscovery in the late 1980s. An obvious influence for George A. Romero's later *Night of the Living Dead* series. Filmed in Salt Lake City. (1962, black and white, not rated.)

CREATURE FROM THE BLACK LAGOON. Strange half-man/half-fish creature (dubbed the "Gill-Man") is discovered in the Amazon River, where it tries to kidnap Julie Adams. The definitive '50s creature feature, this one is hokey in spots, but still fun. Originally in 3-D. (1954, black and white, not rated.)

DR. CYCLOPS. The nasty title character, played with malice by

Albert Dekker, shrinks people in the jungle. Notable mainly for its superior special effects. (1940, color, not rated.)

DR. JEKYLL AND MR. HYDE. There are three versions on video, all of them worth watching. The first is a silent adaptation. A bit hokey at times, but John Barrymore's amazing interpretation (done with facial contortions but no makeup) is well worth a look. The second version, for which Fredric March won an Oscar, is still the best adaptation of Robert Louis Stevenson's yarn about a scientist who develops a formula that brings out the beast in a man. Miriam Hopkins. In the third, Spencer Tracy, Ingrid Bergman, and Lana Turner headline this low-key, slowly paced version, a sort of psychological exploration, which makes it less a horror movie than a character study. (1920/1932/1941, black and white, not rated.)

THE INVISIBLE MAN. The original classic, of course, with a brilliant performance by Claude Rains as a scientist who makes himself invisible and gradually goes mad. Great special effects, even by today's standards. (1933, black and white, not rated.)

JAWS. Steven Spielberg's original is still the best sea-beast movie ever, with excellent performances from Roy Scheider, Richard Dreyfuss, and Robert Shaw, all out to get the great white shark that is chomping up vacationing swimmers. Too gory and frightening for young children. Forget the three sequels. (1975, color, PG, violence, profanity.)

KINGDOM OF THE SPIDERS. This one is no *Arachnophobia,* but it's a surprisingly entertaining yarn about killer tarantulas in Arizona. William Shatner. (1977, color, PG, violence, profanity.)

THE MUMMY. Boris Karloff stars in the title role in what is without peer the best mummy movie ever made, with great makeup and special effects. An ancient Egyptian revived after thousands of years is convinced that a young woman is his reincarnated mate. The Hammer version is also entertaining, with Christopher Lee in the title role and Peter Cushing as the naïve archaeologist who unearths him. (1932, black and white, not rated/1959, color, not rated.)

THE PICTURE OF DORIAN GRAY. The classic interpretation of the familiar Oscar Wilde story, with George Sanders as the man who never ages, though his portrait does. Several color sequences. Donna Reed, Angela Lansbury, Peter Lawford. (1945, black and white/color, not rated.)

THEM! Giant ants in the sewers of Los Angeles! Sounds hokey, but it's actually quite well done. Understated, with a sense of humor and a solid cast of future stars, James Whitmore, James Arness, Fess Parker, and—very briefly—Leonard Nimoy. Edmund Gwenn. (1954, black and white, not rated.)

VILLAGE OF THE DAMNED. Eerie low-budget thriller about mysterious children born in an English village at exactly the same time, who all look alike and have the same emotionless disposition as they grow older. Atmospheric and chilling. George Sanders. (1960, black and white, not rated; the 1964 sequel, *Children of the Damned,* is also on video.)

HUMAN MONSTERS
■■■

THE BAD SEED. Excellent performances (by members of the original Broadway cast) bolster this slightly stagy story of a sweet, innocent young girl (Patty McCormick) who is actually quite evil, killing off those who offend her. Marred somewhat by tacked-on Hollywood ending, but still quite effective. The 1985 TV-remake is not on video. (1956, black and white, not rated.)

FREAKS. Tod Browning's notorious 1932 film is still shocking today, with real deformed carnival "freaks" playing themselves. The story has them getting revenge on a trapeze artist who marries a midget and then tries to poison him for his money. Stiff dialogue delivery hurts some scenes, however. Not for children. (1932, black and white, not rated.)

HUSH . . . HUSH, SWEET CHARLOTTE. Bette Davis and Olivia de Havilland are teamed in this very good, if overlong, shocker about murder and deceit in an old Southern family. Joseph Cotten, Agnes Moorehead, Victor Buono, Mary Astor. Watch young Bruce Dern lose his head in the precredits sequence. (1965, black and white, not rated.)

MIDNIGHT LACE. Doris Day stars in this thriller as an American in London, newly married (to Rex Harrison) and finding herself taunted by a killer. John Gavin, Myrna Loy, Roddy McDowall. The 1980 TV-remake is not on video. (1960, color, not rated.)

MYSTERY OF THE WAX MUSEUM/HOUSE OF WAX. A crazed sculptor covers his victims with wax and shows them off in his museum. Both versions of this yarn are fairly chilling, the first with Lionel Atwill and Fay Wray, the second (originally shown in 3-D) with Vincent Price, Phyllis Kirk, Carolyn Jones, and Charles Bronson. (1933/1953, color, not rated.)

NIGHT OF THE HUNTER. Psycho preacher Robert Mitchum is pure evil in this chiller, marrying Shelley Winters, then stalking his two young stepchildren, who are eventually taken in by protective Lillian Gish. Mitchum delivers a knockout performance in this one. (1955, black and white, not rated.)

THE PHANTOM OF THE OPERA. The original, silent version, with Lon Chaney in top form as the masked composer hiding out in the catacombs of the Paris Opera House, is still the best. The masked ball sequence was filmed in two-strip Technicolor (though some video versions have the scene in black and white). The second one stars Claude Rains, excellent as the Phantom, but it tends to dwell a bit too much on stagebound opera sequences, with warbling Nelson Eddy and Susanna Foster. The 1962 Hammer adaptation and two made-for-TV miniseries versions are not on video. Forget about the gory, R-rated 1989 version. (1925, black and white, not rated/1943, color, not rated.)

SORRY, WRONG NUMBER. Barbara Stanwyck got an Oscar nomination in this expansion of the one-act stage play about a bedridden woman who overhears on the phone that she's about to be murdered. Burt Lancaster. Forget the 1989 made-for-cable-TV remake. (1948, black and white, not rated.)

THE SPIRAL STAIRCASE. Dorothy McGuire is a mute servant in a house full of weirdos, one of whom is a killer. A classic in the Hitchcock mold. Forget the 1975 remake. (1946, black and white, not rated.)

STRAIT-JACKET. Reformed ax-murderess Joan Crawford lives

Lon Chaney, left, and Mary Philbin, right, in the 1925 *Phantom of the Opera.*

peacefully with her daughter (Diane Baker), until more ax mur-ders begin. Naturally, she's the chief suspect. (1964, black and white, not rated.)

WAIT UNTIL DARK. Blind Audrey Hepburn is terrorized by drug dealers Richard Crenna and Jack Weston, not to mention their extremely nasty boss, played with chilling style by Alan Arkin. A knockout chiller. Efrem Zimbalist, Jr. (1967, color, not rated.)

WHAT EVER HAPPENED TO BABY JANE? Bette Davis and Joan Craw-ford are fabulous as aging, battling sisters who were once movie stars. The first of several horror films for each, but by far the best. Forget the made-for-TV remake. Victor Buono. (1962, black and white, not rated.)

COMEDIES

■■■

ABBOTT AND COSTELLO MEET FRANKENSTEIN. Considered by critics the comedy team's finest hour on film, with Bud and Lou meeting up with Frankenstein's monster (Glenn Strange), Dracula (Bela Lugosi), and the Wolf Man (Lon Chaney, Jr.) — and, at the end, even the Invisible Man (Vincent Price). Some riotous bits. (1948, black and white, not rated.)

ARSENIC AND OLD LACE. One of Frank Capra's funniest films (based on a popular Broadway hit), with Cary Grant discovering on Halloween that his kindly old aunts are killers. Some truly hysterical moments. Peter Lorre, Jack Carson, Raymond Massey. (1944, black and white, not rated.)

THE CANTERVILLE GHOST. Charles Laughton stars in this enjoyable tale of the three-hundred-year-old ghost of a man branded a coward, forced to haunt a castle in England until he does something heroic. Margaret O'Brien, Robert Young, Peter Lawford. The 1986 TV remake, with John Gielgud, isn't up to this one (and it tries to be frightening, unlike this version). (1944, black and white, not rated.)

COMEDY OF TERRORS. The casting is better than the script in this dark Roger Corman comedy, with Vincent Price and Peter Lorre as morticians trying to drum up business. Basil Rathbone is a dead man who won't stay dead, and Boris Karloff is Price's hard-of-hearing father-in-law. (1964, color, not rated.)

THE GHOST BREAKERS. Bob Hope and Paulette Goddard confront zombies in a Cuban mansion. A memorable horror comedy. (1940, black and white, not rated. Remade in 1953 by Dean Martin and Jerry Lewis as *Scared Stiff*.)

THE RAVEN. Irreverent Roger Corman spoof about a pair of rival sorcerers, reluctant Vincent Price and nasty Boris Karloff, who are goaded into a duel. (Not to be confused with the 1936 horror thriller by the same name, which also stars Karloff.) Peter Lorre and young Jack Nicholson costar. (1963, color, not rated.)

WONDER MAN. Danny Kaye is very funny as both a bookworm and his show-biz twin brother. The latter is murdered by thugs and returns as a ghost — urging his brother to capture the killers. Virginia Mayo, Vera-Ellen. (1945, color, not rated.)

From left to right: Robert Young, Margaret O'Brien, and Charles Laughton in *The Canterville Ghost*. ©1944 Turner Entertainment Company. All rights reserved. Used by permission.

FOR SMALL FRY
...

BLACKBEARD'S GHOST. Funny Disney fantasy-comedy, with Peter Ustinov as the title character, conjured up by modern-day relative Dean Jones. The pirate helps save his ancient home from mobsters. Suzanne Pleshette, Elsa Lanchester. (1968, color, not rated.)

ESCAPE TO WITCH MOUNTAIN/RETURN TO WITCH MOUNTAIN. In the first movie, evil Ray Milland wants to harness the mysterious powers of two orphan children who are trying to discover where their powers come from. Good Disney effort. Eddie Albert, Don-

144

ald Pleasence. The well-done Disney sequel has Bette Davis and Christopher Lee kidnapping one of the mysterious children to use his powers for their own purposes. (1975/1978, color, G.)

SOMETHING WICKED THIS WAY COMES. Atmospheric chiller from Disney, adapted by Ray Bradbury from his own novel, about a mysterious carnival camping outside a small town and having an odd effect on the townsfolk. Jason Robards, Jonathan Pryce, Diane Ladd, Pam Grier. (1983, color, PG, violence.)

THE WATCHER IN THE WOODS. Disney supernatural thriller has Americans in an English country home haunted by the ghost of a long-dead teenage girl. Bette Davis, Carroll Baker, David McCallum, Lynn-Holly Johnson. (1980, color, PG, violence.)

CHRISTMAS

There are a ridiculous number of Christmas movies shown around the clock on television every November through December, but it's nice to be able to program what you want to watch when you want to watch it. There are probably more videos with a Christmas theme than any other single holiday — including, on several video labels and in varying degrees of quality, that perennial favorite, *It's a Wonderful Life.*

These selections reflect the best that's out there. Even if you've watched them before, they are always welcome again as Christmas rolls around:

TRADITIONAL
...

A CHRISTMAS CAROL. There are many versions available on video but this 1951 effort, with Alastair Sim, is by far the best of the bunch, with a sharp, fine-tuned central performance and great production values. Still, some of the others are pretty good. (1951, black and white, not rated.)

IT'S A WONDERFUL LIFE. Despondent James Stewart is visited by his guardian angel and gets an opportunity to see what life would

145

Donna Reed and Jimmy Stewart (center) in the closing scene of *It's a Wonderful Life*.

have been like if he'd never been born. Stewart is at his best in this Frank Capra classic, as is the supporting cast. Donna Reed, Lionel Barrymore, Thomas Mitchell, Gloria Graham. (1945, black and white, not rated; the TV remake, *It Happened One Christmas*, is not on video; the sequel, *Clarence,* an inferior made-for-TV effort, is.)

MIRACLE ON 34TH STREET. Edmund Gwenn won an Oscar for his wonderful portrayal of an old man who insists he is the real Santa Claus, despite cynical unbelievers in young Natalie Wood and her mother (Maureen O'Hara). John Payne costars. (1947, black and white, not rated; the color TV remake is not on video.)

COMEDIES
■■■

THE BISHOP'S WIFE. A warm, gentle comedy with Cary Grant as an angel assigned to help a bishop (David Niven) and his wife (Loretta Young) get their priorities straight during the holidays. Monty Woolley, Elsa Lanchester. (1947, black and white, not rated.)

CHRISTMAS IN CONNECTICUT. Amusing domestic farce, with Barbara Stanwyck most charming as a phony expert on the art of homemaking. When her boss (Sydney Greenstreet) decides to bring a war hero (Dennis Morgan) to her home for Christmas dinner, she's forced to find a family so she can keep up appearances. (1945, black and white, not rated.)

A CHRISTMAS STORY. Very funny story of a young boy growing up in the 1940s who wants a Red Ryder rifle for Christmas. Perceptive, sometimes hilarious look at life from the viewpoint of a child. Peter Billingsley, Darren McGavin, Melinda Dillon; narrated by screenwriter Jean Shepherd. (1983, color, profanity).

THE CHRISTMAS WIFE. Jason Robards and Julie Harris deliver very good performances in this made-for-cable-TV drama about a lonely man who "hires" a wife for the holidays. (1988, color, not rated.)

ERNEST SAVES CHRISTMAS. The title tells it all. If Ernest P. Worrell (Jim Varney) makes you cringe, forget it, but as "Ernest" films go, this isn't the worst—mainly because it concentrates a bit more on other characters. (1988, color, not rated.)

HOLIDAY AFFAIR. Nice, easygoing romantic comedy has Janet Leigh as a widowed mother, suddenly finding herself courted by two very different men (Robert Mitchum, Wendell Corey). (1949, black and white, not rated.)

THE MAN IN THE SANTA CLAUS SUIT. Fred Astaire is the reason to watch this one. He plays seven roles in this episodic TV comedy, a sort of holiday variation on "The Love Boat." Gary Burghoff, John Byner, Bert Convey, Nanette Fabray, Harold Gould. (1978, color, not rated.)

THE MAN WHO CAME TO DINNER. Hilarious comedy about a pompous radio star who takes over a middle-class household during the holidays, with Monty Woolley recreating his Broadway role. Great cast includes Bette Davis, Jimmy Durante, Ann Sheridan. (1941, black and white, not rated.)

THE NIGHT THEY SAVED CHRISTMAS. Art Carney's lively portrayal of Santa trying to save his toy factory from nearby oil drilling makes this TV movie a delight. Jaclyn Smith, June Lockhart, Paul Williams (as an elf). (1984, color, not rated.)

MUSICALS
∎∎∎

HOLIDAY INN. Though there are several holidays depicted in this terrific musical-comedy, Christmas is the most commonly associated—and why not, since the great Irving Berlin score includes "White Christmas" (which won an Oscar). Bing Crosby and Fred Astaire are a wonderful team. Marjorie Reynolds. (1942, black and white, not rated.)

MARCH OF THE WOODEN SOLDIERS. By far the best of several versions of the Victor Herbert operetta *Babes in Toyland,* a hilarious vehicle for Stan Laurel and Oliver Hardy as incompetent toy shop workers who live among Mother Goose nursery rhyme creatures and who must battle the evil boogeymen. One of Laurel and Hardy's best films. The 1961 Disney version isn't too bad, though the 1986 TV remake is weak; both are titled *Babes in Toyland.* (1938, black and white, not rated.)

WHITE CHRISTMAS. Almost a remake of *Holiday Inn,* with a nice Irving Berlin score (and a reprise of the title tune, of course), along with snappy patter between Bing Crosby and Danny Kaye, and Rosemary Clooney and Vera-Ellen. (1954, color, not rated.)

DRAMA
∎∎∎

THE BEST CHRISTMAS PAGEANT EVER. A very warm TV short film about a social worker (Loretta Swit) staging a Christmas play with delinquent kids. Nicely done. (1978, color, not rated.)

A HOBO'S CHRISTMAS. Lightweight but enjoyable TV drama about an elderly transient (Barnard Hughes) who returns home to the family he deserted twenty years earlier. Gerald McRaney. (1987, color, not rated.)

ONE MAGIC CHRISTMAS. Offbeat but affecting Disney story of a young girl consipiring with an angel (Harry Dean Stanton) to help her mother (Mary Steenburgen) find meaning in Christmas. Moments of stark realism make it a bit harsh for very young children. (1985, color, G.)

PRANCER. Delightful, utterly charming story of an independent

148

young girl (Rebecca Harrell) who believes a wounded reindeer she's found is Santa's Prancer. Meanwhile, her father (Sam Elliott), troubled by financial pressures, is too distracted to pay attention to her. Cloris Leachman. (1989, color, G.)

SANTA CLAUS. Overblown but enjoyable story of the origins of Santa Claus (David Huddleston) is quite good in its first half. The second half loses steam when it switches to the comic story of an elf (Dudley Moore) who defects to an evil toymaker (John Lithgow). Burgess Meredith. (1985, color, PG, violence, profanity.)

THE SHOP AROUND THE CORNER. James Stewart and Margaret Sullivan are squabbling coworkers who don't know they are secretly, romantically corresponding with each other in this terrific Ernst Lubitsch film. (1940, black and white, not rated.)

JUDEO-CHRISTIAN FILMS

Religious films released for general family viewing tend to be more traditional, and the same stories are often told and retold—the lives of Jesus or Moses, Ben-Hur, and others. The times we tend to think of these movies is generally around Christmas or Easter, but they are usually large-scale epics that can be enjoyed any time of year. I have included only those released for the general market:

OLD TESTAMENT
...

THE BIBLE. John Huston directed this anthology of stories from the first twenty-two chapters of Genesis (he also plays a semi-comic Noah in the best of the lot). Slowly paced but interesting. Michael Parks (Adam), Richard Harris (Cain), Stephen Boyd (Nimrod), George C. Scott (Abraham), Ava Gardner (Sarah), Peter O'Toole (three angels). Two tapes. (1966, color, not rated.)

MOSES. This made-for-TV version of the prophet's life, with Burt Lancaster in the title role, is more gritty than DeMille's *The Ten Commandments.* Trimmed from a longer TV miniseries down to feature length, and the gaps sometimes show. May be of interest, however. (1976, color, rated PG, violence.)

THE TEN COMMANDMENTS. Many viewers do not know that Cecil B. DeMille shot two films with this title. The first is an oddly structured, early film. The first half is a stirring, lavish spectacle about the life of Moses (with several scenes in two-strip Technicolor), but the second half is a so-so, overwrought, modern-day story of the wages of sin. The famous remake about the life of Moses, though a bit hokey in places, is still grand epic entertainment, with Charlton Heston heading an all-star cast. Two tapes. (1923, black and white, not rated/1956, color, G.)

NEW TESTAMENT/NEW TESTAMENT PERIOD
■■■

BARABBAS. Anthony Quinn stars as the thief who was released when Jesus replaced him on the cross, following his life thereafter as a gladiator. Rich in spectacle and well-played by Quinn. Arthur Kennedy, Jack Palance, Ernest Borgnine, Katy Jurado. (1962, color, not rated.)

BEN-HUR. Most people think of the Heston film, but there are two fine versions of this movie. The spectacular early version focuses on two friends who grow up together in Imperial Rome, only to become bitter enemies as adults during the time of Christ's ministry, culminating in the famous chariot race. Roman Novarro and Francis X. Bushman are terrific, and the sets and action sequences are knockouts. With a color sequence. The more famous version is fabulous entertainment, an Oscar-winning remake by William Wyler, with Charlton Heston in the title role. It boasts impressive special effects, stirring performances, and that unforgettable chariot race—though some of its impact is lessened on the small screen. Two tapes. (1925, black and white, not rated/1959, color, not rated.)

THE GREATEST STORY EVER TOLD. This epic endeavor by director George Stevens is stirring in some places, dull in others, with spectacular location photography, along with an unfortunate spot-the-star mentality as a parade of well-known faces appear in small roles. Still, Max von Sydow is sincere as Jesus, and Charlton Heston powerful as John the Baptist. Carroll Baker,

Charlton Heston in the chariot-race scene from *Ben-Hur*. ©1959 Turner Entertainment Company. All rights reserved. Used by permission.

Angela Lansbury, Sidney Poitier, Shelley Winters, John Wayne, Telly Savalas, and many others. Two tapes. (1965, color, not rated.)

JESUS OF NAZARETH. Stirring TV miniseries from filmmaker Franco Zeffirelli about the life of Christ, considered by critics the best of the many versions available. All-star cast includes Robert Powell (as Jesus), Anne Bancroft, Ernest Borgnine, James Mason, Laurence Olivier, Christopher Plummer, Rod Steiger, Olivia Hussey. Three tapes. (1976, color, not rated.)

KING OF KINGS. Jeffrey Hunter's portrait of Jesus helps bolster this very well-made, epic version, gorgeously filmed in CinemaScope (which therefore loses some of its impact on the small screen). Robert Ryan. Narrated by Orson Welles. Two tapes. (1961, color, not rated.)

THE KING OF KINGS. H. B. Warner gives a moving performance as Jesus in this early, lavish Cecil B. DeMille production, though some of the other actors are a bit over the top. Still, most worth-

Jeffrey Hunter portraying Jesus Christ in *King of Kings*. ©1961 Turner Entertainment Company. All rights reserved. Used by permission.

while. Silent; resurrection/ascension sequence is in color. (1927, black and white/color, not rated.)

THE ROBE. The wide-screen effects (*The Robe* was the first CinemaScope film) are diminished on television, and the performances are a bit overwrought, but this adaptation of Lloyd C. Douglas's novel about a Roman centurion (Richard Burton) who is changed by the robe that Jesus hands down from the cross is still entertaining. (1953, color, not rated.)

OTHERS
∎∎∎

KEYS OF THE KINGDOM. Gregory Peck had his first major success with this story of a missionary's life (played as a boy by Roddy McDowall). Thomas Mitchell, Vincent Price, Edmund Gwenn. (1944, black and white, not rated.)

A MAN CALLED PETER. Richard Todd's convincing performance

152

as Scotsman Peter Marshall, a minister who became chaplain to the Senate, makes this biographical film. Jean Peters. (1955, color, not rated.)

THE MIRACLE OF OUR LADY OF FATIMA. Touching story of three Portuguese farm kids who see a miracle and find themselves derided by their neighbors. (1952, color, not rated.)

THE SONG OF BERNADETTE. A young peasant girl in the nineteenth-century town of Lourdes, France, sees a vision of the Virgin Mary and finds herself persecuted as a result. Excellent, faith-promoting film won four Oscars, including one for Jennifer Jones in the lead. Charles Bickford, Vincent Price, Lee J. Cobb. (1943, black and white, not rated.)

FOREIGN FILMS

BABETTE'S FEAST. Superbly crafted Oscar-winner as best foreign film of 1987 has two sisters in nineteenth-century Denmark spending their long lives serving others in their small village. Rich in characterization and story. In Danish, with English subtitles. (1987, color, G.)

BEAUTY AND THE BEAST. Lavish classic French version of the oft-filmed tale ranks up there with the greatest movies of all time. The narrative is traditional, but director Jean Cocteau has added surrealistic touches and visual poetry that make for a cinematic feast. In French, with English subtitles. (1946, black and white, not rated.)

CYRANO DE BERGERAC. Gerard Depardieu is magnificent in this rousing adaptation of the classic story of the long-nosed swordsman who helps a friend romance the woman he himself really loves. In French, with English subtitles. (1990, color, PG, violence.)

DRACULA. This version of Bram Stoker's classic tale has a fascinating history, told in a brief prologue on the video—it was made simultaneously with the Bela Lugosi version and shot on the same set at night with a Spanish cast. Bolder than, and in some ways superior to, the Lugosi film. In Spanish, with English subtitles. (1931, black and white, not rated.)

GRAND ILLUSION. Excellent true story of French soldiers in a German POW camp during World War I, plotting their escape; classic antiwar film by Jean Renoir. In French, with English subtitles. (1938, black and white, not rated.)

THE HIDDEN FORTRESS. Akira Kurosawa's action-filled and comical adventure yarn about a stubborn princess and her loyal general crossing dangerous territory, aided by a pair of stumblebums. George Lucas has said this film inspired his *Star Wars* trilogy. In Japanese, with English subtitles. (1958, black and white, not rated.)

MY FATHER'S GLORY/MY MOTHER'S CASTLE. Excellent pair of French films about the childhood memories of author Marcel Pagnol, who grew up a city kid during the early 1900s but fell in love with the country. Charming set-pieces loaded with humor and charm. In French, with English subtitles. (1989, color, G/PG, mature themes.)

RULES OF THE GAME. Jean Renoir's exquisite comedy-drama contrasts the romantic adventures of peasants and aristocrats during a weekend house party. In French, with English subtitles. (1939, black and white, not rated.)

TURKEYS (SO BAD THEY'RE GOOD)

ATTACK OF THE KILLER TOMATOES/RETURN OF THE KILLER TOMATOES/KILLER TOMATOES STRIKE BACK/KILLER TOMATOES EAT FRANCE. Kids are the target audience for these mediocre creature-feature spoofs, which also lampoon bad movies. Some chuckles but not a lot. (1980/1988/1991/1992, color, PG, violence, profanity.)

COMING SOON. Jamie Lee Curtis hosts these clips and theatrical previews for old Universal horror films (*Frankenstein, Dracula,* etc.). Some amusing moments, but mostly for film buffs. Made for video. (1983, black and white/color, not rated.)

Ah! The alien from *Robot Monster* has finally found the last couple on earth. He might have scared them more if he were dressed in a turkey suit.

I WAS A TEENAGE WEREWOLF. Michael Landon got his start as the star of this low-budget yarn that spawned many "I Was . . " teen horror films and spoofs. The title tells all. (1957, black and white, not rated.)

PLAN 9 FROM OUTER SPACE. Often hailed as the worst film of all time, unintentionally hilarious sci-fi thriller with Bela Lugosi (who died during the first week of production) in story of aliens bringing the dead back to life. Watch for those wobbly flying saucers. (1959, black and white, not rated.)

ROBOT MONSTER. Ridiculous yarn about an alien (a man in an ape suit with a diving helmet) who destroys life on earth, save

155

one family that outwits him. Originally in 3-D. (1953, black and white, not rated.)

SANTA CLAUS CONQUERS THE MARTIANS. Seeing young Pia Zadora as a Martian child is the highlight of this silly sci-fi Christmas outing. (1964, color, not rated.)

■ ■

"WHY ISN'T THAT MOVIE ON VIDEO?"
■■■
FRUSTRATIONS OF THE MOVIE FAN

■ ■

The movie questions that most often come my way are whether particular titles are available on video.

For some years the No. 1 most-requested title that remained unreleased was *E.T. The Extra-Terrestrial*. Then Steven Spielberg finally relented and home copies of the film became available. After that, the most sought-after title seemed to be the Cary Grant-Deborah Kerr romance *An Affair to Remember*. That film also belatedly made it to video. Other oft-requested titles that eventually received video releases included Disney's animated classic *Fantasia; Carousel* and *State Fair*, two Rodgers and Hammerstein musicals; *The Party*, a Peter Sellers comedy; *Random Harvest*, an amnesia soap opera with Ronald Colman and Greer Garson; and *How to Murder Your Wife*, a Jack Lemmon farce.

Several Disney animated features are still not available, including *Snow White and the Seven Dwarfs* — which the studio says is the only one that will likely never see the light of video — *Song of the South*, *The Aristocats*, *The Fox and the Hound*, *The Black Cauldron*, and *Oliver & Company*. However, the Disney folks have their own unique master plan for releasing a couple of animated features on video each year.

In addition, there are many other beloved older movies

that haven't yet made their way to the market simply because the studios that own them don't give "golden oldies"
the same priority as more recent productions, regardless
of quality. Why? Because of profit motives based on Hollywood's love affair with the largest demographic group
of video renters — teenagers — who, by and large, would
rather watch any newer movie in color than a film that is
in black and white or is more than five years old.

Consequently, we see a myriad of generically titled
clunkers that never made it into general theatrical release
being shuttled to video every month. Sure, the big hits
always head quickly to the home video market, but week
after week we also see such trash as *Barbarian Queen II* and
Mindwarp slotted into video store shelves while old favorites continue to gather dust in studio warehouses. Too bad
the Hollywood decision makers don't realize that many
older movies — some of them bona fide classics — have a
rabid following, people who would happily dip into their
entertainment bucks to rent or buy them.

The one major movie studio that has made a conscious
effort to release numerous titles from its archives on a
regular basis is MGM-UA, a library now owned by Ted
Turner. Say what you want about Turner the entrepreneur,
Turner the film librarian has turned out to be a hero to
movie lovers, pioneering what is easily the largest regular
releasing schedule of old movies on video. The other studios let a few older titles trickle out here and there but at
an agonizingly slow pace.

Are you listening, Hollywood? The list that follows is
composed of the most requested movies that are not on
video at the moment but that movie fans would most like
to rent or buy. These movies have built-in audiences ready
to help your profits rise. And, despite the fact that some
are considered by the critics to be clunkers, they are among
the most frequently requested, and they were still unavailable when this book went to press:

THE MOST-REQUESTED TITLES
(IN ORDER OF POPULARITY)

MCLINTOCK!/HONDO/ISLAND IN THE SKY/THE HIGH AND THE MIGHTY.
These four John Wayne movies are in the custody of the late
star's son, Michael Wayne. All are in video limbo, and they won't
even show up on television until the younger Wayne decides to
cut them loose. *McLintock!* (1963) is unquestionably the No. 1
most-requested title, a slapstick Western with Maureen O'Hara;
Hondo (1953), action Western with Geraldine Page (originally in
3-D); *Island in the Sky* (1953), a World War II survival melodrama;
The High and the Mighty (1954), the first multiple-character airborn
disaster flick, with Laraine Day.

THE SLIPPER AND THE ROSE. Not-bad musical adaptation of *Cinderella,* with Richard Chamberlain. (1976.)

THE PROMISE. Kathleen Quinlan is very good in this silly soap
opera about a young woman whose boyfriend's mother will pay
for her plastic surgery after an accident only if she agrees to play
dead. (1979.)

LOST HORIZON. The later musical version starring Liv Ullmann
and Peter Finch, with songs by Burt Bacharach and Hal David.
(1973.)

ANNIE GET YOUR GUN. This terrific musical, starring Betty Hutton
and Howard Keel, is tied up in the Irving Berlin estate and is
simply unavailable—even to TV. (1950.)

BRIGHAM YOUNG. The epic film about Mormon pioneers, with
Dean Jagger in the title role, Vincent Price as Joseph Smith, and
young romance provided by high-profile stars Tyrone Power
and Linda Darnell. (1940.)

CHEAPER BY THE DOZEN/BELLES ON THEIR TOES. Delightful domestic comedies starring Myrna Loy and, in the first one, Clifton
Webb. (1950/1952.)

OF MICE AND MEN. Burgess Meredith is George, and Lon Chaney,
Jr., is Lenny in this sensitive, heartwrenching adaptation of the
Steinbeck classic. (1939.)

IT HAPPENS EVERY SPRING/ANGELS IN THE OUTFIELD. Pair of base-ball comedies, the first about a chemist (Ray Milland) who comes up with a way to make baseballs avoid bats and the second about heavenly intervention helping the Pittsburgh Pirates. (1949/1951.)

KNOCK ON WOOD. Danny Kaye in one of his better films, as a neurotic ventriloquist mixed up with spies in London. (1954.)

SUPPORT YOUR LOCAL GUNFIGHTER. James Garner and Suzanne Pleshette star in this easy-going follow-up—but not sequel—to *Support Your Local Sheriff.* (1971.)

ELEANOR AND FRANKLIN/ELEANOR AND FRANKLIN: THE WHITE HOUSE YEARS. Two superb Emmy-winning miniseries starring Jan Alexander and Edward Herrmann. (1976/1977.)

FREQUENTLY REQUESTED
(ALPHABETICALLY)

ABBOTT AND COSTELLO MEET THE MUMMY/IT AIN'T HAY/HERE COME THE CO-EDS. Although twenty-four of Bud Abbott and Lou Costello's thirty-six movies are now on video (along with Costello's only solo film), fans invariably ask about titles not yet released. The best of the unavailable are probably *It Ain't Hay* (1943) and *Here Come the Co-Eds* (1945), but *Abbott and Costello Meet the Mummy* (1955) is the most requested.

ADVANCE TO THE REAR. Glenn Ford stars in this Civil War farce, with Stella Stevens, Melvyn Douglas, Joan Blondell, and Jim Backus. (1964.)

ALL THAT HEAVEN ALLOWS. Good soap opera of widow Jane Wyman taking up with young man Rock Hudson, despite local gossip. (1955.)

ANNA AND THE KING OF SIAM. Irene Dunne is Anna and Rex Harrison is the king in this adaptation of the book that later served as the basis for *The King and I.* (1946.)

THE ART OF LOVE. Carl Reiner's comedy about an American artist

160

(Dick Van Dyke) in Paris who plays dead so his buddy (James Garner) can "find" his newly valuable paintings. (1965.)

THE BEAR. Not the one about a bear, but the one about Paul "Bear" Bryant, the college football coach, starring Gary Busey and Harry Dean Stanton. (1984.)

THE BLISS OF MRS. BLOSSOM. Offbeat romantic comedy, a British film, with Shirley MacLaine and Richard Attenborough. (1968.)

THE BOURNE IDENTITY. Richard Chamberlain stars in this TV miniseries adaptation of the Robert Ludlum best-seller. Jaclyn Smith. (1988.)

BREEZY. Clint Eastwood directed (but does not appear in) this May-December romance, with William Holden and Kay Lenz. (1973.)

THE CAT AND THE CANARY. One of Bob Hope's best films, the one that established him as a movie star. An "old, dark house" yarn, a memorable horror comedy costarring Paulette Goddard. (1939.)

A CHRISTMAS CAROL. George C. Scott stars in this made-for-TV version that shows up on television every other year. And every Christmas this becomes a much asked-about item. (1984.)

DARLING LILI. Julie Andrews in an underrated musical spy yarn set against World War II, with Rock Hudson. (1970.)

DEANNA DURBIN. Only one of Durbin's films (*It's a Date*) is on video, but her many movies, especially the early musicals, are often requested.

DRACULA. The British made-for-TV version starring Louis Jourdan, which shows up from time to time on PBS stations (usually around Halloween). (1978.)

FITZWILLY. Dick Van Dyke is a stuffy butler who organizes a heist of Gimbel's, for humanitarian reasons, of course. (1967.)

A FOREIGN AFFAIR. Billy Wilder's great comedy with Jean Arthur and Marlene Dietrich, an underrated gem. (1948.)

FORTY POUNDS OF TROUBLE. *Little Miss Marker* clone stars Tony Curtis, Suzanne Pleshette, Phil Silvers, Stubby Kaye. (1963.)

FRANCIS THE TALKING MULE. Of Universal's seven *Francis* films, only *Francis in the Navy* is available. (1949–1956.)

THE GHOST AND MR. CHICKEN. Don Knotts's haunted house comedy is asked about every Halloween. (1966.)

GOODBYE, CHARLIE. A gangster is bumped off, then reincarnated as Debbie Reynolds in this farce. Tony Curtis, Pat Boone, Walter Matthau. (1964.)

HELLZAPOPPIN. Hilarious Ole Olsen and Chic Johnson farce composed of dozens of off-the-wall, disconnected skits, based on the comedy team's Broadway hit. (1941.)

THE INNOCENTS. Scary adaptation of Henry James's *The Turn of the Screw,* starring Deborah Kerr and Michael Redgrave. (1961.)

J. W. COOP/THE HONKERS. Two solid rodeo films about over-the-hill riders going out for one more run at the circuit; the more current *My Heroes Have Always Been Cowboys* has prompted a recent rise in interest. (1972/1972.)

LAWMAN. Burt Lancaster in a cerebral Western, with Robert Ryan, Robert Duvall. (1971.)

MA AND PA KETTLE. None of the nine films in this Universal series are on video, though you can get the movie that introduced Marjorie Main and Percy Kilbride as these characters, *The Egg and I.* (1949–1957.)

ME AND THE COLONEL. Danny Kaye's first straight role, more or less, was in this light satire about a Jew and a German officer forced to rely on each other during World War II. (1958.)

MERRY ANDREW. Kaye again, this time in a romantic comedy with a circus backdrop. (1958.)

THE MINIVER STORY. The sequel to *Mrs. Miniver,* with Greer Garson and Walter Pidgeon reprising their roles. (1950.)

MR. BUDDWING. Amnesiac James Garner tries to figure out who he is in New York City, with help from Jean Simmons, Angela Lansbury, Katharine Ross, and Suzanne Pleshette. (1966.)

MOVE OVER, DARLING. Doris Day and James Garner star in this remake of the comedy *My Favorite Wife.* (1963.)

MURDER, HE SAYS. Very funny farce about innocent Fred MacMurray finding himself in a house full of hillbilly killers. (1945.)

NOSFERATU–THE VAMPYRE. Werner Herzog's moody German Dracula tale, with Klaus Kinski and Isabelle Adjani, a great, low-key horror film. (1979.)

O. HENRY'S FULL HOUSE. Remembered primarily as a holiday film, this anthology of five of the author's twist-ending yarns (including *The Gift of the Magi* and *The Last Leaf*) has five different directors (Howard Hawks among them) and an all-star cast (Charles Laughton, Richard Widmark, Marilyn Monroe, Fred Allen). Hosted by John Steinbeck. (1952.)

ONIONHEAD. Andy Griffith is in the Coast Guard in this attempt to cash in on his *No Time for Sergeants* success. Felicia Farr, Walter Matthau, Joey Bishop. (1958.)

OTHELLO. Laurence Olivier's superbly acted version of Shakespeare's classic. (1965.)

PORGY AND BESS. This musical boasts some of George and Ira Gershwin's best songs, starring Sidney Poitier, Dorothy Dandridge, Pearl Bailey, Sammy Davis, Jr., Diahann Carroll. This one is tied up in the Gershwin estate and isn't shown on TV anymore either. (1959.)

ROBINSON CRUSOE. Luis Bunuel's classic film version of the Daniel Defoe tale, with Dan O'Herlihy (who was nominated for an Oscar). (1952.)

ROBINSON CRUSOE ON MARS. Science fiction fans know this terrific little space twist on the Defoe yarn. (1964.)

SAILOR BEWARE/LIVING IT UP/YOU'RE NEVER TOO YOUNG. Only seven of Dean Martin and Jerry Lewis's sixteen films as a team are on video, but their best, including these three, remain on the studio shelf. (1951/1954/1955.)

SECONDS. Arguably, Rock Hudson's best performance is his role here as a businessman who gets a new life—literally. (1966.)

163

THE SHEPHERD OF THE HILLS. John Wayne stars in this story of life in the Ozarks, with a great supporting cast of veteran character actors. (1941.)

STAR! Film biography of Gertrude Lawrence, starring Julie Andrews. (1968.)

SWISS FAMILY ROBINSON. Freddie Bartholomew, Thomas Mitchell, and Edna Best star in this adaptation of the novel, narrated by Orson Welles. (1940.)

VALLEY OF DECISION. Greer Garson is a maid working in the home of a Pittsburgh industrialist, falling for the family's son, Gregory Peck. (1945.)

THE WILD NORTH. Stewart Granger is an accused murderer pursued by relentless Mountie Wendell Corey in this thriller. Cyd Charisse. (1952.)

YOU NEVER CAN TELL. A dog is murdered and finds himself reincarnated as detective Dick Powell, searching for the killer in this zany comedy. (1951.)

SUBJECT INDEX

Action/adventure movies, 89–92; for children, 103; with wartime themes, 127–28. *See also* Westerns
"Airline cuts" (edited versions of movies), 29–31
Altman, Robert, 87
Anderson, Hans Christian, 58, 113
Animal stories, 100–103
Animated features: combined with live action, 85, 86, 111, 117–18; Western, 98; by Walt Disney, 111–14; by Don Bluth, 115; featuring "Peanuts" characters, 115; miscellaneous, 116–17
Attenborough, Richard, 78
Austen, Jane, 77

Baseball movies, 125–26
Berlin, Irving, 80, 85, 88, 148
Bernstein, Leonard, 85
Bible, films based on, 149–52
Big as example, 30
Biographies, film: general category, 72–74; miscellaneous biographies, 46, 48, 87–88, 89, 152–53; sports biographies, 126–27
Black-and-white movies: defense of, 36–37; list of short comedic, 39–42
Bluth, Don, 115
British comedies, 54–55
Broadway musicals adapted for screen, 81–85
Brontë, Charlotte, 76
Browning, Tod, 140

Capp, Al, 83
Capra, Frank, 55–56, 120, 143, 146
Carroll, Lewis, 111–12
Chaney, Lon (biography), 73
Children: advertising misdirected toward, 19–20; offensive material in films aimed at, 20–22
Children's movies: animals, 100–103; circus themes, 108; domestic comedy, 109; drama, 109–10; fantasy/science fiction, 103–7; Halloween/horror, 144–45; Muppets, 107; outdoor adventure, 103; Shirley Temple, 108–9. *See also* Animated features
Christian films, 149–53
Christie, Agatha, 121–23
Christmas movies, 145–49
Circus movies, 108
Classification and Rating Administration (CARA), 12, 15, 18
Cocteau, Jean, 153
Cohan, George, 89
Colorization, 36–37
Comedies: black-and-white shorts, 39–42; British, 54–55; Frank Capra, 55–56; Charlie Chaplin, 56; Christmas themes, 146–47; domestic, 51–53, 109; ghosts or spirits, 53–54; Halloween/horror, 142–44; Buster Keaton, 57; miscellaneous, 57–61; "screwball," 49–51; wartime

165

INDEX OF ACTORS AND ACTRESSES

179

189

INDEX OF MOVIE TITLES

196